AF327041

Logic Design
for
Behavioral Scientists

Logic Design

for

Behavioral Scientists

Roy Udolf, Ph.D.

Professional-Technical Series
Nelson-Hall Company

ISBN: 0-911012-54-0
Library of Congress Catalog Card Number: 73-75522

To my students, past, present, and future, who have always made the frustrations and irritants of academia seem trivial.

Contents

Acknowledgments

The following are some of the people to whom the author is indebted for help in the preparation of this book:

Philip E. Burton whose excellent lectures inspired this work.

Mary Joan DeMarco who typed the entire manuscript.

Marian Anthony and Caroline Rountree who had the Herculean task of proofreading the manuscript.

Dr. Hadassah Paul and Matthew Frankfort for their reading of the entire text and their many helpful comments.

The author, however, reserves to himself full credit for any remaining errors or omissions, since he did not incorporate every improvement suggested.

Preface

Every book needs a specific goal to justify its existence and the investment of the reader's valuable time that it requires.

The specific goal of this book is to provide a sound theoretical and practical background in logic devices and design for intelligent, professional people who are not engineers. It is not intended as another oversimplified logic design cookbook that assumes that the reader is mentally defective or that the theory of logic design is so complicated that only an electronic engineer can understand it fully. The problem with the latter approach is that by trying to oversimplify logic design the material is usually made more obtuse. Aside from this, the reader of such a book is not prepared to use his own creative ability to implement designs that are not specifically illustrated or to adapt given designs to different applications.

This book attempts, in a series of short chapters, to acquaint the reader with the basic theory of all the major types of logical devices and their use in logic system design. The chapters have been kept as short as possible, and each builds on the preceding ones to cover some major area of logic design.

While this book is intended primarily for behavioral scientists, it is hoped that the material will be useful to anyone involved with logic design, including engineers who have never been involved with this area.

While the book aims at a basic understanding of principles, a high school physics course should provide sufficient background for understanding the material.

Logic Design

for

Behavioral Scientists

Chapter 1
Introduction to Logic Systems

A system is a collection of components that function together to produce some desired result. Systems may be as commonplace as bicycles or automobiles or as esoteric as an ICBM. They may vary in complexity from a simple wheel and axle to a modern computer containing millions of components. The human skeleton, a wristwatch, and the entire judicial system of the United States are all properly classified as systems.

The kind of systems that will be dealt with in this book is a subclass of systems called electronic systems. These are systems in which the component parts consist of circuitry, mechanical devices, or any combination thereof.

The system specifications (or specs) define what inputs are to be fed into the system and what outputs the system is required to generate from these inputs. In other words, a system specification is a series of statements concerning the relationships between input and output variables. It defines exactly what tasks the system is to perform, under what environmental conditions, and with what degree of precision or accuracy.

The first step in designing any system is for the system designer to write a detailed set of system specifications. These specifications are based on the task requirements of the system—i.e., what it is supposed to do.

The system, if it is at all complex, is then usually broken down into a series of simpler constituent subsystems, or components, which are usually referred to by engineers as "black boxes." The term "black box" results from the fact that the system designer is really not concerned with what is inside the component as long as it meets the specifications, or input-output statements, that he has assigned to it. The same specifications can be met by a wide variety of individual circuitry, and from the systems point of view the specific circuits used are irrelevant as long as the specifications are met.

When a system is broken down into a collection of black boxes, the system engineer writes a separate set of specifications or functional requirements for each black box. Very often black box specifications will require a greater overall accuracy than system specifications, to allow for a buildup of tolerances.

Figure 1–1(a) shows a hi-fi system with its basic requirements, and Figure 1–1(b) shows how this could be broken down into a collection of black boxes. Each black box, having been assigned its own speci-

INPUT
(RECORD DISC)
HI FI SYSTEM
OUTPUT
(SOUND)
A

HI FI SYSTEM
CONTROLS
INPUT
TURNTABLE
AMPLIFIER
SPEAKER
OUTPUT
POWER
SUPPLY
POWER
INPUT
B

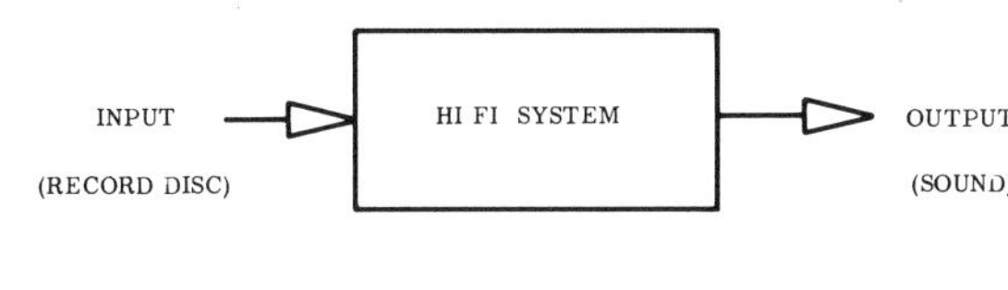

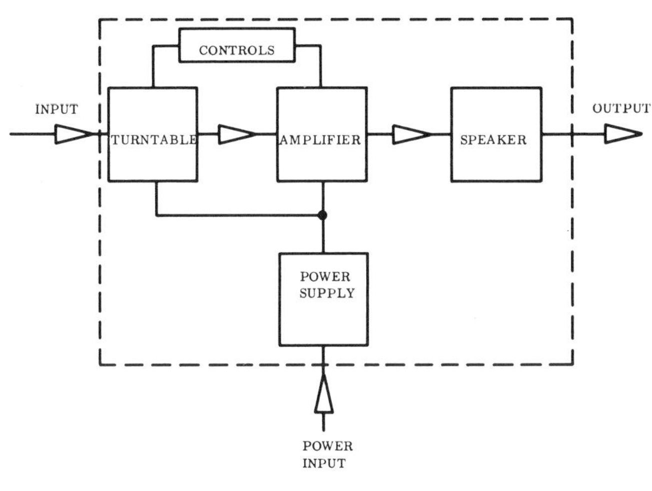

Figure 1–1

fication requirements, will in general be designed by a different specialist. If the system engineer has done his job well and if each black box meets its own specifications, then all of the black boxes will function correctly when the system is assembled; i.e., the system will be within specifications.

Thus, in ordinary electronic system design each component black box requires a circuit designer to design special circuits needed to meet the special requirements of the component specifications.

In the case of logic systems, this is not the case. Here there are a few basic circuit designs that are used over and over, and system design consists merely of putting these basic building blocks into the correct juxtaposition.

A logic designer needs very little knowledge of circuit design, since the basic circuits are not only trivial but they are usually available commercially as predesigned packages. These basic building blocks are sold in compatible sets and commonly utilize μ logic or integrated circuit chips which are both inexpensive and subminiature.

Therefore, it is possible to design quite sophisticated logic systems and translate these designs into workable hardware with very little knowledge of basic electronics. The theory and techniques of this design and what it can do for the experimental apparatus designer will be the subject of the following chapters.

A logic system is a special type of system that is made of components that can be in only one of two possible states at any instant of time. This is the essential difference between a logic system and what is called a proportional or analogue system wherein a given component may have an infinite variety of states. For example, an amplifier may produce an output voltage of from 0 to 10 volts and have any intermediate value at a given instant of time, but a logic system component may exist in only one of two possible states, usually referred to as 0 and 1 respectively. Thus, logic systems are also called binary systems, which is a more descriptive term.

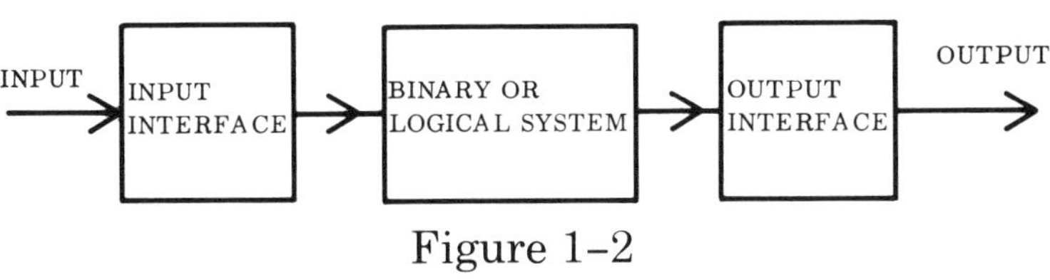

Figure 1–2

Most logic systems are designed to operate from input signals different from those used in the logic devices and yield outputs at different levels than binary devices. Therefore, they must contain components called interfacing devices that convert external inputs into binary signals of proper magnitude and convert binary outputs into a form suitable to work external devices. Figure 1–2 shows the essentials of a logic system and its required interfacing devices in block diagram form.

A logic system is of interest to the designers of experimental equipment because it provides a simple and inexpensive way of automatically controlling or programing a large variety of experimental routines.

It can, for example, do all of the following things plus a great deal more:

1. Accurately time sequential program steps utilizing the same or different time intervals between steps.
2. Make future program steps contingent on a response or a given number of responses.
3. Provide a branching function wherein the next step in a program is a function of subject response.
4. Sequentially program a series of stimuli.
5. Record responses.
6. Any combination of the foregoing.

Chapter 2
Basic Concepts in Logic Design

The name logic design results from the work of George Boole. Around 1850, Boole designed a form of algebra, now called Boolean algebra, which was intended to solve logic problems such as syllogisms. A syllogism is a statement of an "If–Then" relationship. Classically there are two "If" statements, called the premises (A and B), and a "then" statement or a conclusion (Z). For example,

Premises:	A	All lions are mammals.
	B	This animal is a lion.
Conclusion:	Z	Therefore this animal is a mammal.

A syllogism is valid *if* when the premises are true *then* the conclusion must be. It should be noted that the validity of a syllogism is a matter of form rather than fact, since the conclusion can be false, if the premises are, and the syllogism may still be valid.

This type of problem deals with two basic types

of conditions—true or false, or valid or invalid—which can be symbolized by the following notation:

$$0 - \text{false}$$
$$1 - \text{true}$$

It is important to realize that 0 and 1 as used here are *not* numbers but states of truth.

It is not the intention of this book to deal with logic problems per se, but to show how these basic ideas have been given modern applications far removed from the original type of problems that classical logicians have dealt with.

Because a logic system deals with two and only two basic conditions or states, it is an extremely useful type of system in terms of hardware. For example, in a proportional system, where there are many possible states of inputs and outputs, a vacuum tube becomes useless once its emission falls below that portion of the operating curve over which it is being used. However, in a digital, or two state, system, the components are either conducting or not and they have much longer life expectancies.

As will be shown later, the 10-character number system that we are all familiar with has nothing magic about it. It may have resulted from the simple fact that people have ten fingers. Instead of the decimal system, other number systems could be used having more or less than 10 characters. A number system having only two characters, 0 and 1, is called a binary system, and this system is often used so that the advantages of two state design can be used in arithmetic computing devices.

Thus, sometimes 0 and 1 may represent logic states in a system and at other times they may represent binary numbers. It will be important to keep clearly in mind which condition obtains in all design work.

In view of the foregoing, a logic system is always a binary system and has only two possible states, 0 or 1. In terms of hardware these two states may be represented in a variety of ways, as shown in Figure 2–1. At any instant of time these devices can be in only one of two states and *in no other.*

In general a logic system may consist of any number of inputs and outputs. Conventionally, input signals are represented by the initial letters of the alphabet, and outputs are represented by the final letters of the alphabet.

Figure 2–2 shows the simplest logic system possible having only one input and one output. A, being a binary signal, can be either in the 0 state or the 1 state. The same is true of output Z.

Z is a function of A; i.e., the value of Z depends on what the value of A is and what is inside the black box. This is denoted by $Z = f(A)$ (read: "Z is a function of A"). Thus, whether Z is a 1 or a 0 is determined by whether A is a 1 or a 0 and what the system does to A to produce Z. The transformation that is accomplished by the black box is what is meant by a function.

What functions are possible in a binary or two

DEVICE	0	1
SWITCH		
RELAY		
ELECTRON TUBE OR TRANSISTOR	CUT OFF	SATURATED
MAGNETIC CORE	SATURATED N	SATURATED S
FLIP FLOP	STATE # 1	STATE # 2

Figure 2-1

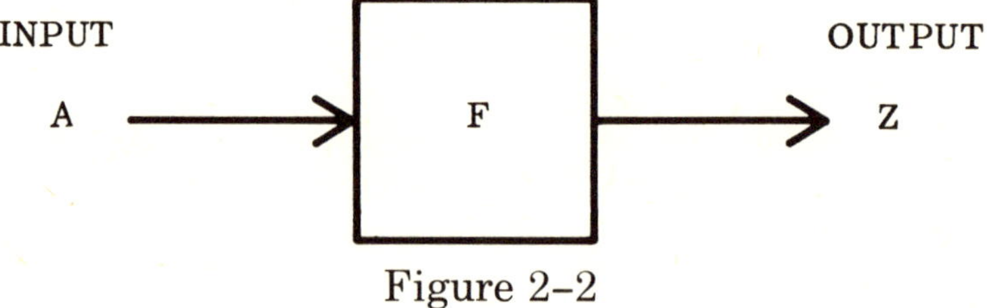

Figure 2-2

state system will now be investigated. Also which of these functions are basic (i.e., which functions can be combined to produce all of the others) will also be investigated.

In a One Input System
If when $A = 0$ then $Z = 0$
and when $A = 1$ then $Z = 1$

then the function is a simple statement of A or an assertion of A. This can be attained in terms of hardware by a permanently connected (or "hard wired") wire between the input and output, as shown in Figure 2–3.

If when $A = 0$ then $Z = 1$
and when $A = 1$ then $Z = 0$

then the function is called a *not* function or a logic inversion or a negation. It is represented symbolically by a small circle, as shown in Figure 2–4, and is denoted by the symbol $\overline{A}$ which is read "not A."

The negation function is one of the three basic functions used in practical design work. It is directly analogous to the phase inversion produced by electron tubes; therefore to obtain a negation function always requires some active device like a tube or a transistor. Hence, the negation circle always appears in conjunction with some other symbol and never alone. $\overline{A}$ is also called the complement of A.

If $Z = 0$ when $A = 0$ or 1, the function is called the null set. If $Z = 1$ when $A = 0$ or 1, the function is called the universe set. In either of these two cases,

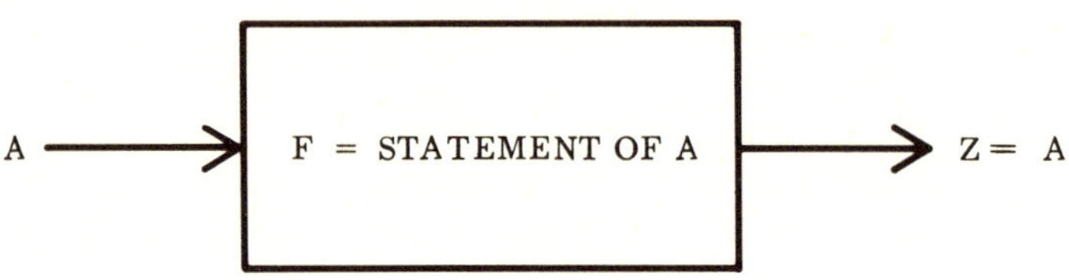

LET:

$$1 = +6 \text{ V}$$

$$0 = 0 \text{ V}$$

THEN:

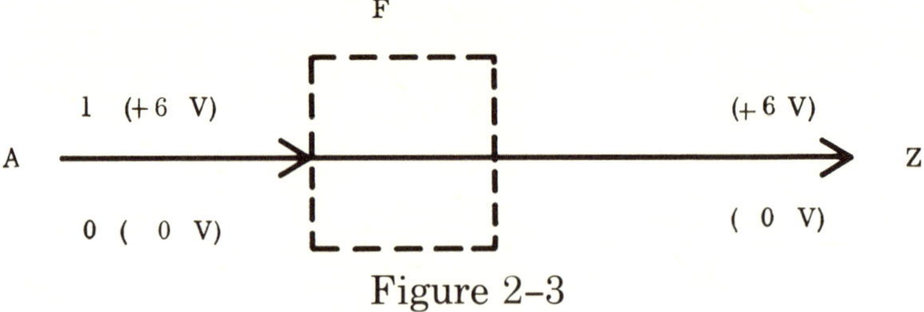

Figure 2–3

A
F = NOT
(NEGATION)
Z = $\overline{A}$

A
$\overline{A}$
OR
A
$\overline{A}$
OR
A
$\overline{A}$

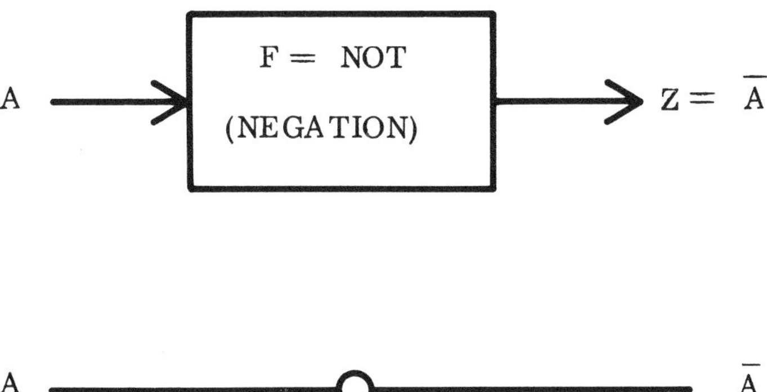

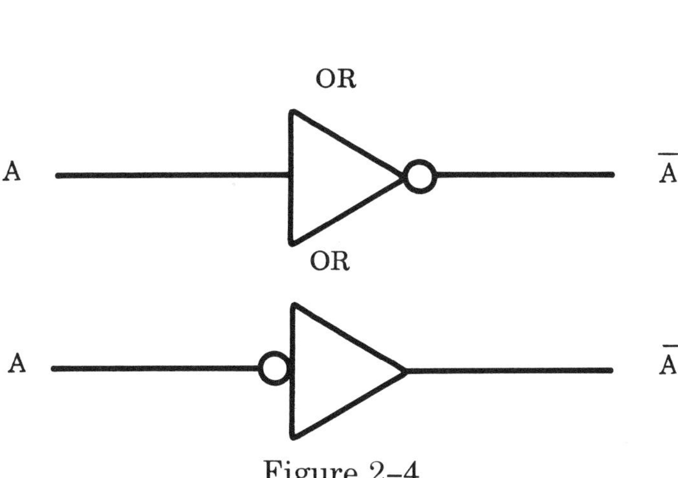

Figure 2–4

Z does not depend for its value on the value of A, and is a constant.

The next more complex logic system involves two inputs, A and B, as shown in Figure 2–5. It is now necessary to consider the four possible permutations of input states. This is conventionally done by writing these possible states in an orderly manner as follows:

State	0	1	2	3
A	0	1	0	1
B	0	0	1	1

This representation of the possible states (0, 1, 2, 3, etc.) is called the standard basis. For the three input variable system of Figure 2–6, the standard basis would look like:

State	0	1	2	3	4	5	6	7
A	0	1	0	1	0	1	0	1
B	0	0	1	1	0	0	1	1
C	0	0	0	0	1	1	1	1

Notice that with each additional input variable the number of permutations of input states doubles. The total number of input states is 2^N, where N is the number of input variables. Thus, for a four input system there would be 2^4 or 16 input state permutations, and the standard basis showing these 16 possibilities would look as follows:

State	0	1	2	3	4	5	6	7	8	9	10	11	12	13	14	15
A	0	1	0	1	0	1	0	1	0	1	0	1	0	1	0	1
B	0	0	1	1	0	0	1	1	0	0	1	1	0	0	1	1
C	0	0	0	0	1	1	1	1	0	0	0	0	1	1	1	1
D	0	0	0	0	0	0	0	0	1	1	1	1	1	1	1	1

The foregoing matrices represent all possible combinations of input conditions in a given system.

Now some of the possible binary functions of two input systems will be considered.

If $Z = 1$ when both A and $B = 1$ and $Z = 0$ in all

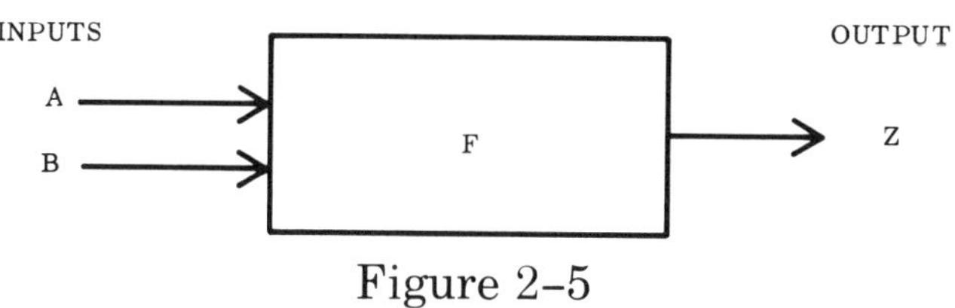

Figure 2–5

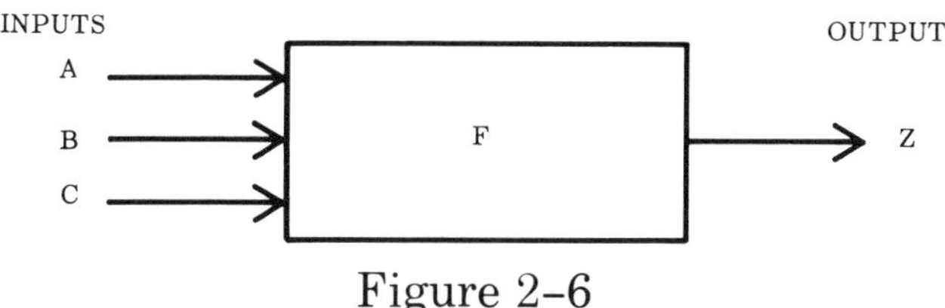

Figure 2–6

other cases, the function is called an *and* function; this is the second basic function that logic designers constantly use. The *and* function can be represented with the standard basis for a two input system as follows:

State	0	1	2	3
A	0	1	0	1
B	0	0	1	1
Z	0	0	0	1

This diagram, or truth table as it is called, shows that $Z = 1$ when and only when both A and B are in the 1 state and $Z = 0$ for all other combinations of the states of A and B. The *and* function is written $A \cdot B$ or just AB and is read "A and B," not "A times B." This is logical, not arithmetic, multiplication.

The component of hardware that produces this function is called an "*and* gate" and is symbolized on logic diagrams as shown in Figure 2–7. Figure 2–7 also shows how an *and* function can be attained in terms of hardware by two switches or relay contacts wired in series.

It can be seen that in order to get an output from the two switches both must be in the 1 or closed state.

The third and final basic building block in logic systems is the *or* gate. If $Z = 1$ when either A or B or both are 1 and $Z = 0$ when both A and B are 0, the function is called the *or* function. The following truth table defines the *or* function:

State	0	1	2	3
A	0	1	0	1
B	0	0	1	1
Z	0	1	1	1

By now it should be obvious that a truth table is in fact a specification for a logic function since it defines the value of the output Z for all possible combinations of inputs.

The *or* function is denoted $A + B$ and is read "A or B," not "A plus B." Again this is logical, not arithmetic, addition. About the only difficult thing that the beginning logic designer has to do is to extinguish past habits and learn that $AB = A$ *and* B and that $A + B = A$ *or* B.

Figure 2–8 shows the symbol used for an *or* gate on logic diagrams. It also shows how an *or* gate can be attained in terms of hardware by two switches or relays wired in parallel. An output will be obtained here if either or both switches are closed.

It will be noted that an *and* gate corresponds to a conjunctive concept and an *or* gate corresponds to a disjunctive concept.

While for certain practical reasons, which will be discussed later, other basic building blocks are commonly utilized in actual hardware, most logic

AND GATE

A

B

Z = AB

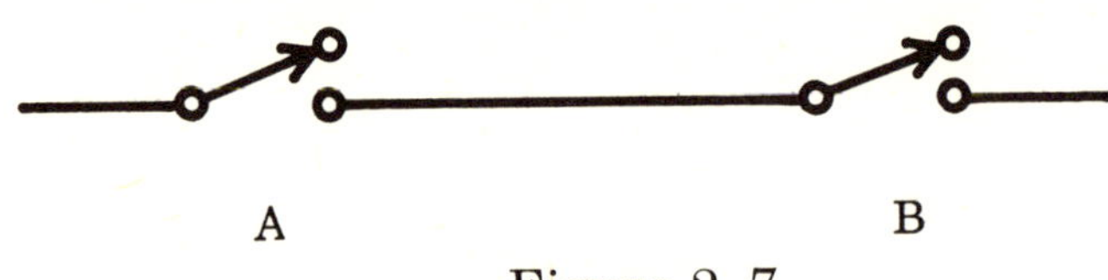

Figure 2-7

OR GATE

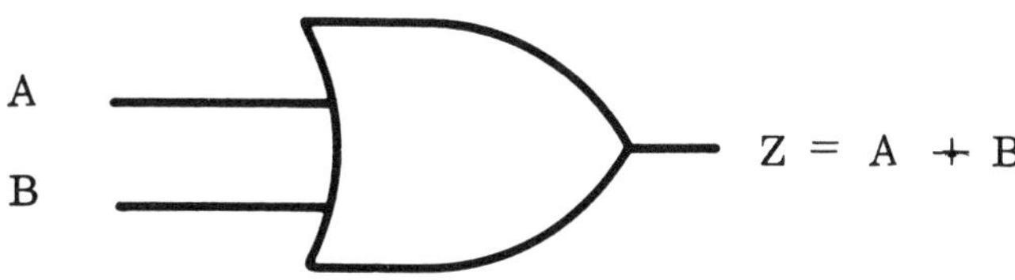

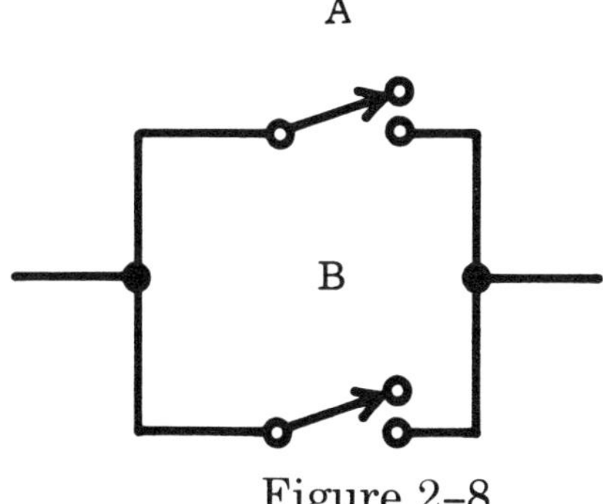

Figure 2–8

design problems can be solved with the three basic functions of *not, and,* and *or.*

The following truth table defines a less commonly used function called the *exclusive or,* which is denoted as $A \oplus B$:

State	0	1	2	3
A	0	1	0	1
B	0	0	1	1
Z	0	1	1	0

As can be seen from the truth table, the *exclusive or* function gives a 1 output when either A or B but not both is 1. The logic symbol for the *exclusive or* function is shown in Figure 2–9.

EXCLUSIVE OR GATE

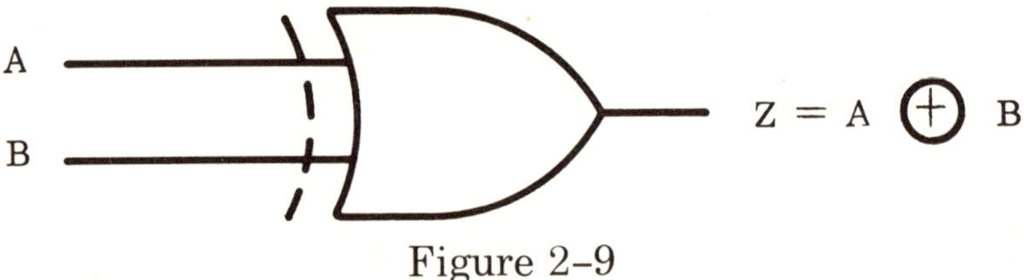

Figure 2–9

It is obvious that if the input state possibilities are written in the standard basis format, and only if they are written in this format, the number shown for the output states of Z will be unique for each possible logic function, and this particular sequence of 0's and 1's will designate this particular function. Hence, it is called a designation number (#).

Before going further, it is necessary to expand the idea of an *and* or an *or* gate to systems involving three or more inputs. Table 2–1 shows the designation numbers for the *and, or,* and *exclusive or* functions in a three input variable system, and Figure

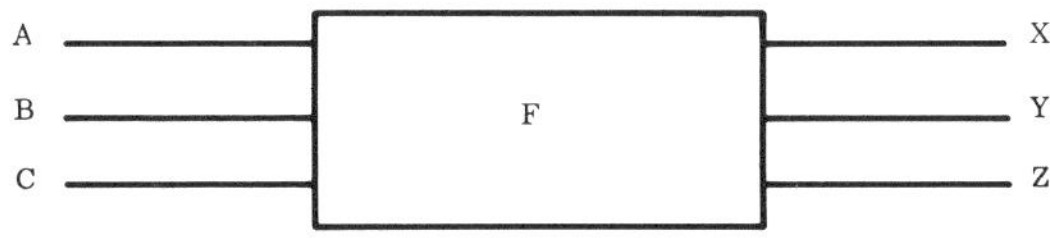

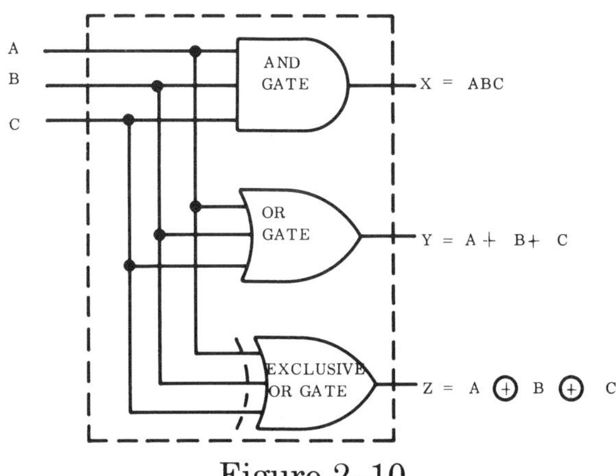

Figure 2–10

2–10 shows the symbols used for these three types of gates.

Table 2–1

State	0	1	2	3	4	5	6	7	
A	0	1	0	1	0	1	0	1	
B	0	0	1	1	0	0	1	1	
C	0	0	0	0	1	1	1	1	
X	0	0	0	0	0	0	0	1	*And* $X = ABC$
Y	0	1	1	1	1	1	1	1	*or* $Y = A + B + C$
Z	0	1	1	0	1	0	0	0	*exclusive or*
									$Z = A \oplus B \oplus C$

In a multi input system the *not* function can be applied to either individual variables or combinations of variables. Table 2–2 shows some of the *not* functions for a two input system. $\overline{A} \cdot \overline{B}$ is read "not A and not B." $\overline{AB}$ is read "not the quantity A and B."

Table 2–2

State	0	1	2	3
A	0	1	0	1
B	0	0	1	1
$\overline{A}$	1	0	1	0
$\overline{B}$	1	1	0	0
AB	0	0	0	1
$\overline{AB}$	1	1	1	0
$A + B$	0	1	1	1
$\overline{A + B}$	1	0	0	0
$\overline{A} \cdot \overline{B}$	1	0	0	0
$\overline{A} + \overline{B}$	1	1	1	0

Note that $\overline{A} \cdot \overline{B} \neq \overline{AB}$ and $\overline{A} + \overline{B} \neq \overline{A + B}$.

Two logic functions are equal or equivalent if and only if their designation numbers are identical. The foregoing inequalities can be demonstrated by looking at the designation numbers in the above table. If two logic functions have identical designation numbers they are equivalent, and one can replace the other with no change in system performance.

Chapter 3
Additional Concepts in Logic Design

It was shown in the previous chapter that two logic functions are equal or equivalent if and only if they have identical designation numbers. However, it will not always be apparent by inspection whether two logical expressions are equivalent or not. To test for equality, write the designation number for each expression. For example, to prove the identity

$$ABC \equiv ABC(A + B)$$

write the designation number for each side of the equation as shown in Table 3-1.

Table 3-1

State	0	1	2	3	4	5	6	7	
A	0	1	0	1	0	1	0	1	
B	0	0	1	1	0	0	1	1	
C	0	0	0	0	1	1	1	1	
(1) ABC	0	0	0	0	0	0	0	1	
(2) $A + B$	0	1	1	1	1	1	1	1	Equal
(3) $ABC(A + B)$	0	0	0	0	0	0	0	1	

(Note: Treat lines 1 and 2 as single variables and *and* them.)

The reader will notice that this illustrates the general technique for finding designation numbers of complex Boolean expressions. The designation numbers are obtained for the simpler expressions and combined, state by state, according to the rules of logical addition and multiplication.

Due to the isomorphism, or similarity of form, it is obvious that if the identity $ABC \equiv ABC(A+B)$ has been proven then the identity $ABC \equiv ABC(B+C)$ is also true.

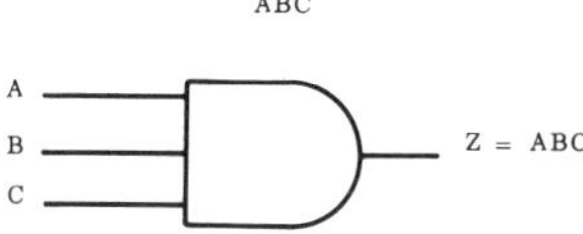

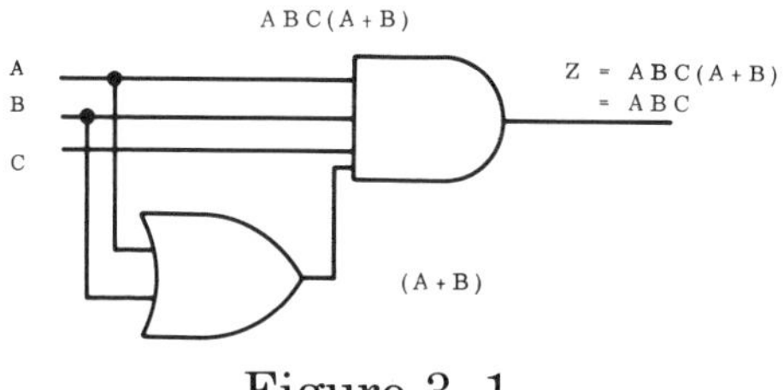

Figure 3–1

Figure 3–1 shows the logic diagrams representing the two equivalent expressions ABC and $ABC(A + B)$. This figure illustrates something very significant. Both of the logic diagrams produce exactly the same result, but the first requires only a single *and* gate while the second requires two gates, one *and* and one *or*. Thus, there is more than one way to skin the same cat. To design the simplest and therefore the most economical and reliable hardware, it is essential to express the logical statements in the simplest form possible. Techniques for doing this will be explained in Chapter 9.

If it is possible for many different appearing logic statements to be functionally equivalent, the question naturally arises as to how many truly different logic functions, i.e., having different designation numbers, are possible in a given situation. The number of different logic statements possible is a function of the number of input signals.

As has been shown, there are 2^N different possible combinations of input states in the standard basis where N is the number of inputs. Since each possible input state contributes one digit to the designation number and this digit has two possible states, 1 or 0, it follows that there are 2^{2^N} different binary functions possible.

Thus, for a one input system there are four different functions as follows:

State	0	1	
A	0	1	Function
	0	0	Null Set = Constant 0
	0	1	Statement of A
	1	0	Not A = Complement of A = Negation of A
	1	1	Universe = Constant 1

For a two input system there are 16 basic functions as shown in Table 3–2.

The reader who is already familiar with binary numbers will notice that the designation numbers of these 16 functions are the binary numbers from 0 to 15 written in order. Figure 3–2 shows logic diagrams for all of the above basic functions in terms of the basic *and, or,* and *not* gates. (Except the first and the last which are simply permanent 0 or 1 states that are independent of the input signals, and *A* and *B* which are simply lines representing hard wires to the input variables.)

Some of the functions shown in Figure 3–2 are worthy of comment. For example, Figure 3–2(b) shows the function $\bar{A}B$, "not *A and B*." This is called "*A* inhibits *B*" because if *A* is 1 when *B* is 1 there will be a 0 output. The same situation obtains in Figure 3–2(c) where *B* is shown to inhibit *A*.

Figure 3–2(d) shows that an *exclusive or* function can be attained by means of two *and* gates and an *or* gate. A study of all of these figures discloses that any of these unique functions can be generated from the proper combinations of the *and, or,* and *not* functions.

Figure 3–2(f) shows the *nor* or *not or* function. It will be noted that when an individual input is negated the *not* symbol appears on the appropriate input line, but in the case where the entire expression is negated the *not* symbol appears on the output line.

Figure 3–2(g) is called an equivalence function

Table 3–2

State	0	1	2	3	
A	0	1	0	1	
B	0	0	1	1	Function
	0	0	0	0	$0 = $ Constant
	0	0	0	1	$AB = $ And
	0	0	1	0	$\overline{A}B = A$ inhibits B
	0	0	1	1	$B = $ Input
	0	1	0	0	$A\overline{B} = B$ inhibits A
	0	1	0	1	$A = $ Other input
	0	1	1	0	$A\overline{B} + \overline{A}B = $ Exclusive or
	0	1	1	1	$A + B = $ Or
	1	0	0	0	$\overline{A + B} = $ Nor (i.e., not or)
	1	0	0	1	$AB + \overline{A} \cdot \overline{B} = $ Equivalence or $A = B$
	1	0	1	0	$\overline{A} = $ Complement of $A = $ not A
	1	0	1	1	$\overline{A} + B = $ Implication
	1	1	0	0	$\overline{B} = $ Complement of $B = $ not B
	1	1	0	1	$A + \overline{B} = $ Implication
	1	1	1	0	$\overline{AB} = $ Nand (i.e., not and)
	1	1	1	1	$1 = $ Constant

because in order to get a 1 output both A and B must be in the same state, i.e., either both 0 or both 1. Note this is different from the *and* function where both A and B must be 1 to get an output of 1.

Beyond the three basic functions of *and, or,* and *not,* the foregoing unique functions of two input variables contain two important new types of gates, the nand and the nor. As shown in Figures 3–2(l) and 3–2(f), a nand gate is formed by negating the output of an *and* gate, and a nor gate is formed by negating the output of an *or* gate. As a practical matter most logic design is worked out in terms of

A
B
Z = AB
# 0001
AND
A

A
B
Z = A̅B
# 0010
A INHIBITS B
B

A
B
Z = AB̅
# 0100
B INHIBITS A
C

A
B
Z = AB̅ + BA̅
# 0110
EXCLUSIVE OR
D

A
B
Z = A + B
# 0111
OR
E

A
B
Z = A̅ + B̅
# 1000
NOR
F

A
B
Z = AB + A̅B̅
# 1001
EQUIVALANCE
G

A
Z = A̅
# 1010
A
H

A
B
Z = A̅ + B
# 1011
IMPLICATION
I

B
Z = B̅
# 1100
B
J

A
B
Z = A + B̅
# 1101
IMPLICATION
K

A
B
Z = A̅B̅
# 1110
NAND
L

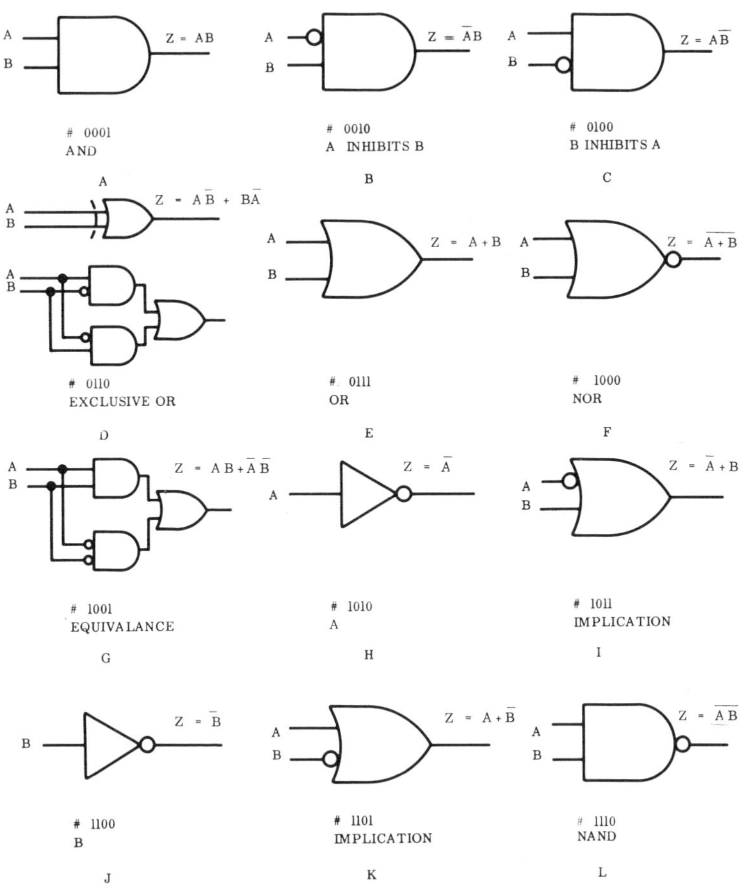

Figure 3-2

and and *or* logic for simplicity's sake, but then the design is finally implemented in terms of nand or nor gates for reasons of practical circuit considerations. How *and-or* logic can be mechanically converted into nand or nor logic will be shown later.

Before proceeding further, it might be desirable to give the reader some feeling for how the concepts developed thus far can be applied to simple practical problems. In terms of experimental apparatus, binary input signals may be taken to represent conditions precedent having the two possible states of being present or absent. For example, consider a Skinner box having a red and a green light each worked by a separate on-off switch. Suppose that it is desired to wire these lights in such a manner that the red light will always be turned on if the green light is or if its own switch is on.

Let A = the red light switch

$\qquad B$ = the green light switch

To solve this problem (i.e., design a circuit meeting these requirements or specs),

1. write a logic statement of these requirements, and
2. translate this logic statement into hardware.

To accomplish the first step, write out the possible permutations of the inputs in the standard basis as follows:

A (Red Switch)	0	1	0	1
B (Green Switch)	0	0	1	1

Then complete the truth table by writing the designation number of the required outputs. This is done by considering each combination of input states individually and deciding what level each output must be at for each of these input states.

A (Red Switch)	0	1	0	1	
B (Green Switch)	0	0	1	1	
x Red Light	0	1	1	1	$A + B$
y Green Light	0	0	1	1	B

Designation numbers are now available for the required outputs for the red and green lights. The logic diagram for a system with the above two inputs and two outputs would therefore look as shown in Figure 3–3(a).

If the logic level of 0 is represented by an open switch and the logic level of 1 is represented by a closed switch, the logic diagram could be translated into hardware as shown in Figure 3–3(b).

Obviously this trivial circuit could have been designed directly without the intervention of logic design. However, these techniques can be used to simplify very complex system requirements and can reduce hardware design to simple mechanical steps.

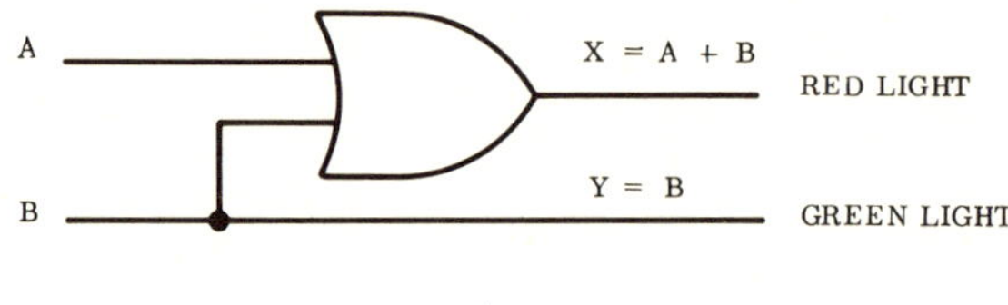

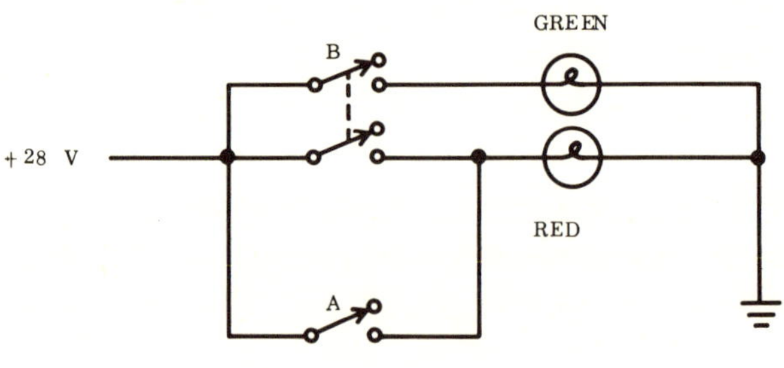

Figure 3–3

Chapter 4
Boolean Algebra

A logical identity, like a trigonometric identity, is an equation or a statement of equality that holds true for all possible values of the variables. To illustrate, $2X + 3 = 7$ is an equation. This statement is only true for one particular value of the variable X, i.e., when $X = 2$. For all other possible values of X, the statement is not true. Solving an equation means to find the particular value or values of X for which the statement of equality is true.

The statement $\sin^2\theta + \cos^2\theta \equiv 1$ is an identity. It is true for whatever possible value is assigned to angle θ. Thus, an identity is a special type of equation which is universally true.

In a two input variable system, there are certain important identities which enable the logic designer to simplify logic statements and thereby translate them into the simplest possible hardware.

Note that in each of these four identities there is an *and* gate with four possible permutations of

Identities Involving One Variable or One Variable and a Constant

And Identities

$$(1) \; A \cdot \overline{A} \equiv 0$$
$$(2) \; A \cdot A \equiv A$$
$$(3) \; A \cdot 0 \equiv 0$$
$$(4) \; A \cdot 1 \equiv A$$

two inputs. A 0 or a 1 refers to a constant or non-variable input state.

In the first identity, whatever state A is in, i.e., 0 or 1, $\overline{A}$ must always be in the opposite state. Hence, there will never be two 1 level inputs, and the output of the *and* gate must always be 0.

In the second identity, whenever A is 1 there will be two 1 level inputs and hence a 1 level output, while whenever A is 0 there will be two 0 inputs and hence the output of an *and* gate will be 0. Thus, the output state will always be equal to A.

In the third identity, if one input to the *and* gate is constantly 0 the output must always be 0 regardless of the state of A.

In the final identity, if one input to an *and* gate is constantly 1 then the output will be 1 when A is 1 and 0 when A is 0; hence it will be equal to A.

It should be obvious from the isomorphism or similarity of form involved that if the foregoing identities are true then the following identities are equally valid:

And Identities
$$B \cdot \overline{B} = 0$$
$$B \cdot B \equiv B$$
$$B \cdot 0 \equiv 0$$
$$B \cdot 1 \equiv B$$

It may not be so obvious, but these identities also hold for aggregates of variables.

Let $A = [AB(C + D)]$ in a four input system.

Then, by identity 1: $A \cdot \overline{A} \equiv 0$

or: $[AB(C + D)] \cdot [\overline{AB(C + D)}] \equiv 0$

Or Identities
$$(5)\ A + \overline{A} \equiv 1$$
$$(6)\ A + A \equiv A$$
$$(7)\ A + 0 \equiv A$$
$$(8)\ A + 1 \equiv 1$$

Again these identities hold for any single variable in a system and for aggregates of variables.

In the first case, since an *or* gate is involved it is apparent that whatever condition variable A is in, at least one of the two possible conditions for a 1 output will be present, and hence the output will be constantly 1. In other words this gate could be replaced with a hard wired 1 signal.

In the second identity, the 1 level on each of the two input lines must occur together or not at all. Hence, the output will be the same as the state of A.

Note that the same results will obtain in the third situation for we are dealing here with an *or* gate which means that only one input must be a 1 to get a 1 output.

In the last identity, since there is a constant 1 input it follows that the output must always be 1, and this gate can be replaced by a hard wired 1 level signal.

It may now be apparent that the value of these identities is in simplifying hardware. For example, identities 5 and 8 show that an *or* gate may be replaced with a plain permanent wire to a 1 source, and identities 6 and 7 show that an *or* gate in these situations is equivalent to a connection to signal A directly. Also *and* gate identities 1 and 3 reduce an *and* gate to a permanent connection to a constant 0 level signal, and identities 2 and 4 eliminate an *and* gate in favor of a connection to input signal A.

It is possible to simplify more complex expressions and generate further identities by considering combinations of the foregoing eight identities. For example,

$$\left.\begin{array}{l} A\overline{A} \equiv A0 \quad\ \equiv 0 \\ A + \overline{A} \equiv A + 1 \equiv 1 \end{array}\right\} = \text{constant}$$

$$A + A \equiv A + 0 \equiv AA \equiv A1 \equiv A$$

Also the above identities imply a set of inequality statements; e.g.,

$$A\overline{A} \neq A + \overline{A} \text{ etc.}$$

Another useful identity arises by definition:

$$\textit{Not Identity}$$
$$(9)\ \overline{\overline{A}} \equiv A$$

IDENTITIES INVOLVING TWO OR MORE VARIABLES

(10) $A + B \equiv B + A$ commutative law for logical addition

(11) $A \cdot B \equiv B \cdot A$ commutative law for logical multiplication

(12) $AB + AC \equiv A(B + C)$ distributive law

(13) $A + \overline{A}B \equiv A + B$

Identities 10 and 11 are obvious from the nature of *or* and *and* gates. The general method of demonstrating the validity of an identity will now be shown using identity 12 as an example, and the validation of identity 13 will be left as an exercise for the reader.

As might be suspected, the way of showing that the right and left sides of identity 12 are equivalent will be to find the designation number for each expression and show that they are identical. In other words, it will be shown that for any possible input state permutation each statement produces the identical output state—which is what is meant by the equality of logic.

The proof is begun by writing the standard basis for all possible combinations of states of A, B, and C. Then the designation numbers for the basic elements of each statement are written and combined into larger units in accordance with the logic statements given until the designation number of each side of the equation is attained. Finally, the two designation numbers obtained are compared as follows:

$$AB + AC \equiv A(B + C)$$

Read: "A and B, or A and C equals A and, B or C."

A	0	1	0	1	0	1	0	1
B	0	0	1	1	0	0	1	1
C	0	0	0	0	1	1	1	1
$[AB + AC]$								
(1) AB	0	0	0	1	0	0	0	1
(2) AC	0	0	0	0	0	1	0	1
(3) $AB + AC$ (1) + (2)	0	0	0	1	0	1	0	1
$[A(B + C)]$								
(4) A	0	1	0	1	0	1	0	1
(5) $B + C$	0	0	1	1	1	1	1	1
(6) $A(B + C)$ (4) · (5)	0	0	0	1	0	1	0	1

Comparison of the designation numbers on lines 3 and 6 shows them to be identical, QED.

It will be noted that the designation numbers for the functions AB and AC are different from each other and are also different from the designation number 0001 which was the *and* function for AB in a two variable system. This last statement is due to the fact that here the truth table represents a three input variable system.

Figure 4–1 shows the logic diagrams for each side of the identity. These two logic diagrams have just been demonstrated to be functionally identical. It is apparent that the right-hand side of the identity is simpler to implement than the left-hand side since it requires only two gates, one *and* and one

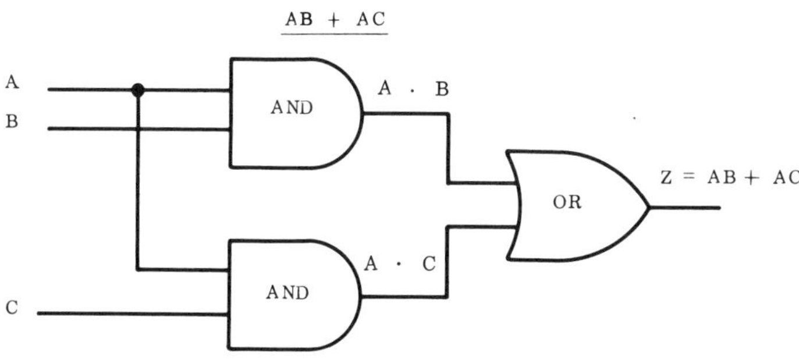

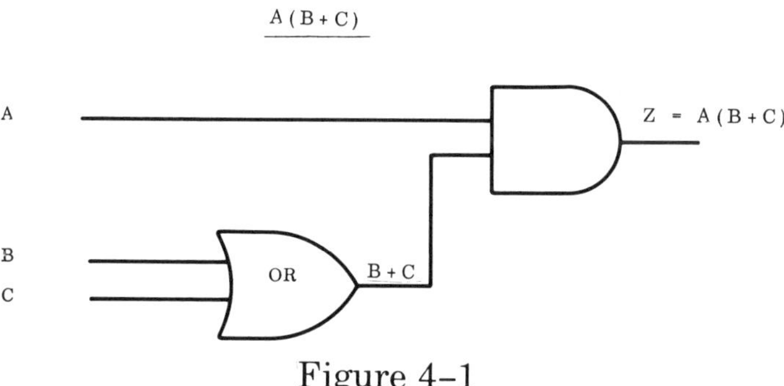

Figure 4-1

or, while the functionally identical left-hand side of the identity requires three gates to implement, two *and's* and one *or.*

The foregoing identities were dealt with here to familiarize the reader with the language of logic design and to illustrate the extremely important idea that while the same function can be accomplished in an infinite variety of ways, only one of these possibilities is the simplest possible and therefore the cheapest and best method.

Chapter 5
DeMorgan's Theorems

There are two Boolean identities that are of basic importance. They are constantly used in converting easy to write logic statements, written in terms of *and* and *or* gates, into logic statements written in terms of nand or nor gates, which is the form that is usually implemented into hardware. These are called DeMorgan's theorems and are the following:

$$(1)\ \overline{AB} \equiv \overline{A} + \overline{B}$$
$$(2)\ \overline{A + B} \equiv \overline{A} \cdot \overline{B}$$

Identity 1 states that the *not and* or *nand* function is equivalent to an *or* gate with the inputs negated.

Identity 2 states that the *not or* or *nor* function is equivalent to an *and* gate with the inputs negated.

Notice that the *not* bar on the left side of both equations negates the entire expression while on the right side of both equations the negation sign is applied to each variable individually.

Figure 5–1 shows the equivalences of the logic symbols involved.

The first identity will now be proven, and it will be left as an exercise for the reader to prove the second.

$$\overline{AB} \equiv \overline{A} + \overline{B}$$

A	0	1	0	1
B	0	0	1	1
(1) AB	0	0	0	1
(2) $\overline{AB}$	1	1	1	0
(3) $\overline{A}$	1	0	1	0
(4) $\overline{B}$	1	1	0	0
(5) $\overline{A} + \overline{B}$	1	1	1	0

Line 2 has the identical designation number as line 5, QED.

Like all of the identities discussed, DeMorgan's theorems apply to aggregates of variables as well as to individual variables. To apply DeMorgan's theorem to a complex expression it is merely necessary to:

1. Remove the negation bar over the entire expression if one is present or add it if it is absent.
2. Negate each individual variable in the expression.
3. Change the *or* signs to *and* signs or vice versa.

1) $\overline{AB} = \overline{A} + \overline{B}$
A
B
NAND
$\overline{AB}$
=
A
B
OR
$\overline{A} + \overline{B}$

2) $\overline{A+B} = \overline{A} \cdot \overline{B}$
A
B
NOR
$\overline{A + B}$
=
A
B
AND
$\overline{A} \cdot \overline{B}$

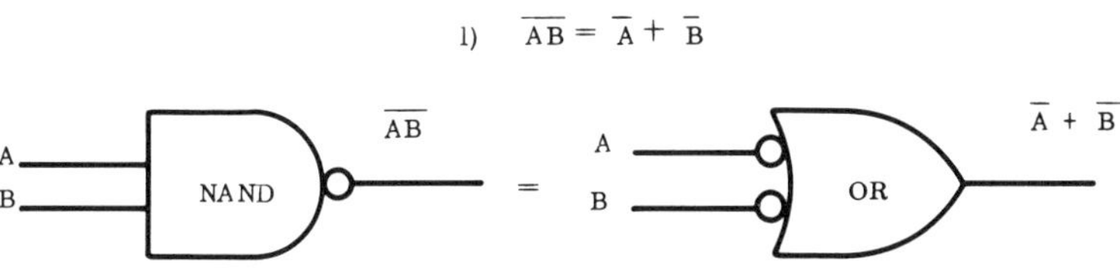

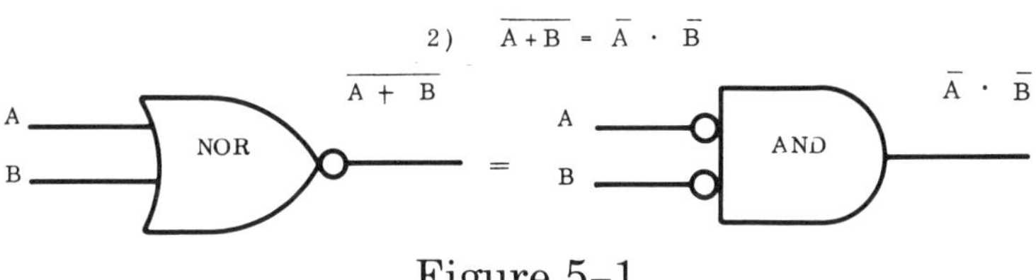

Figure 5-1

Example 1:   DeMorganize $\overline{A \cdot \overline{B} + C \cdot \overline{D}}$

Note: Here the "A" in identity (2) $= A \cdot \overline{B}$ and the "B" $= C \cdot \overline{D}$.

$$(1)\ \ A \cdot \overline{B} + C \cdot \overline{D}$$
$$(2)\ \ \overline{A} \cdot B + \overline{C} \cdot D$$
$$(3)\ \ (\overline{A} + B) \cdot (\overline{C} + D)$$

Example 2:   DeMorganize $(\overline{A} + B) \cdot C$

$$(1)\ \ \overline{(\overline{A} + B) \cdot C}$$

$$(2)\ \ \overline{(A + \overline{B}) \cdot \overline{C}}$$

$$(3)\ \ \overline{(A \cdot \overline{B}) + \overline{C}}$$

To prove $(\overline{A} + B) \cdot C = \overline{(A \cdot \overline{B}) + \overline{C}}$, construct the following table:

A	0	1	0	1	0	1	0	1
B	0	0	1	1	0	0	1	1
C	0	0	0	0	1	1	1	1
(1) $\overline{A}$	1	0	1	0	1	0	1	0
(2) $(\overline{A} + B)$	1	0	1	1	1	0	1	1
(3) $(\overline{A} + B) \cdot C$	0	0	0	0	1	0	1	1
(4) $\overline{B}$	1	1	0	0	1	1	0	0
(5) $(A \cdot \overline{B})$	0	1	0	0	0	1	0	0
(6) $\overline{C}$	1	1	1	1	0	0	0	0
(7) $(A \cdot \overline{B}) + \overline{C}$	1	1	1	1	0	1	0	0
(8) $\overline{(A \cdot \overline{B}) + \overline{C}}$	0	0	0	0	1	0	1	1

Line 3 = line 8, QED.

At this stage the reader should be able to draw a logic flow diagram directly from a logic statement or function, or go in the opposite direction and write a logic statement directly from a logic diagram.

The best technique for doing the former is to read the logic statement in words.

For example, draw a logic diagram for the following statement:

$$Z = (AB\overline{C} + A\overline{B}) \cdot D$$

This is read: "Z equals A and B and not C, or A and not B, and D."

As can be seen from the function, there must be two *and* gates, one with three inputs $(AB\overline{C})$ and one with two inputs $(A\overline{B})$. In each case, one of the inputs must be negated. The outputs of these gates must then become the input to an *or* gate. Finally the output of the *or* gate must be *and*ed with D for the final output. Thus, the diagram of Figure 5–2 results.

It will be realized that this statement and its diagram is just one of an entire family of equivalent statements. It has been written in terms of *and − or* logic since this is the simplest and most direct way, but having obtained the original statement it might be desirable to implement it in terms of the more practical *nand* or *nor* logic. There are two steps that would be taken in this case:

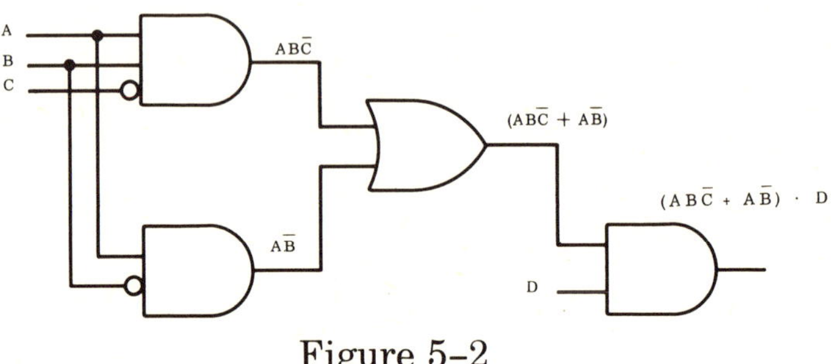

Figure 5-2

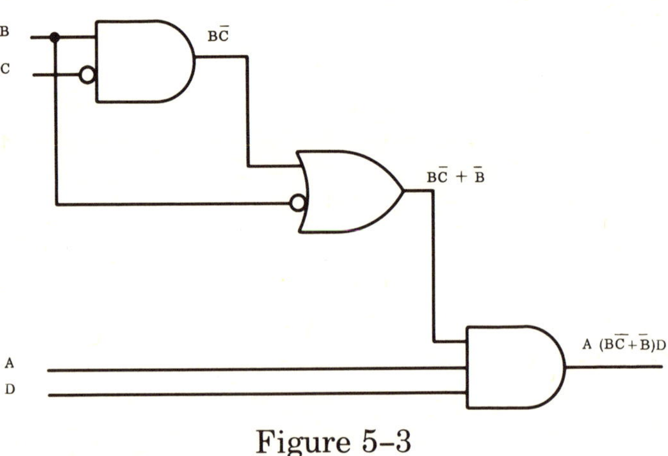

Figure 5-3

1. **Simplify** the statement as much as possible using the Boolean identities (although sometimes simplifications will be obvious from a perusal of the logic diagram).
2. **DeMorganize** it to convert from *and–or* to nand or nor logic.

Step 1

If $Z = (AB\overline{C} + A\overline{B}) \cdot D$, then by factoring out the A in the bracketed term we get:

$$Z = A(B\overline{C} + \overline{B})D$$

In terms of *and-or* logic this reduces the four gate logic diagram of Figure 5–2 to the three gate diagram of Figure 5–3.

Step 2

To DeMorganize $A(B\overline{C} + \overline{B})D$, write:

$$(1)\ \ \overline{A(B\overline{C} + \overline{B})D}$$
$$(2)\ \ \overline{\overline{A}(\overline{B}C + B)\overline{D}}$$
$$(3)\ \ \overline{\overline{A} + ([\overline{B} + C] \cdot B) + \overline{D}}$$

The negation bar over the entire expression shows that we are noring the three major terms $\overline{A}$, $([\overline{B} + C] \cdot B)$, and $\overline{D}$. This can be seen in Figure 5–4.

It will be noted that Figure 5–4 involves a mixture of *nor, or,* and *and* gates. This is undesirable

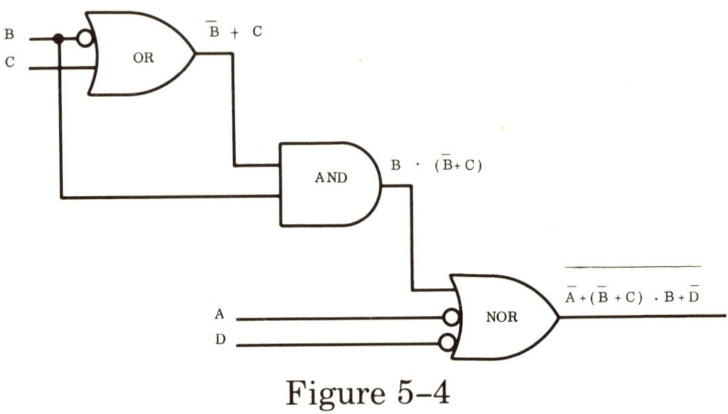

Figure 5–4

as ultimately we are going to use commercially available logic chips which will include only nand or nor functions, thus the logic must be further converted. More specifically, the remaining *and* and *or* gates must be converted to nor gates. The general technique to do this is exactly the same as has been used. Start from the output end, i.e., the most complex expression, and keep DeMorganizing by working toward the simplest functions. In the present case the most complex function that remains to be converted is: $B(\overline{B} + C)$. DeMorganizing this we get:

$$(1)\ \overline{B(\overline{B} + C)}$$
$$(2)\ \overline{\overline{B}(B + \overline{C})}$$
$$(3)\ \overline{\overline{B} + B\overline{C}}$$

It will be obvious that (3) is a nor gate, noring the functions $\overline{B}$ and $\overline{BC}$.

The last function to be converted is the simple one, $B\overline{C}$, which by the same technique reduces to

$$\overline{\overline{B} + C}$$

or a nor gate.

Figure 5–5 shows the completed conversion of the partially converted diagram of Figure 5–4. The reader should compare this with the directly written logic of Figure 5–2 with which it is functionally identical.

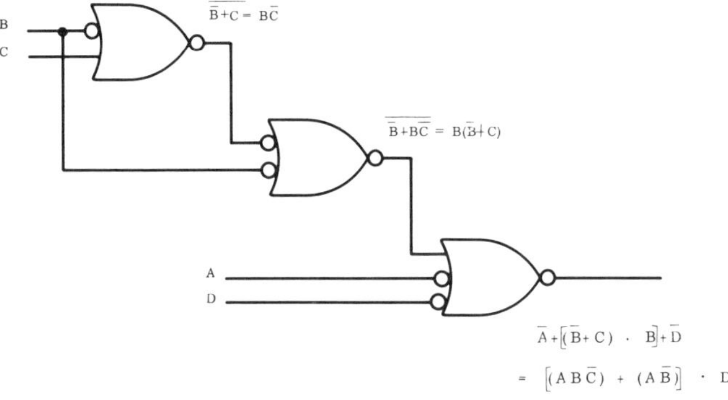

Figure 5–5

In comparing Figures 5–5 and 5–2 it will be noticed that the original logic statement required four gates to implement, three *ands* and an *or*. The simplified and converted logic required only three gates, three nors. In both cases three stages were required. A stage refers to the sequential gates that a signal must pass through from input to output. Sometimes in simplifying logic the number of gates may be reduced at the cost of increasing the number of stages or sequential steps necessary. As yet in this discussion nothing has been said concerning time. All of the input and output signals have been considered as steady state affairs that are permanently in the 1 or 0 state. Later, when the dimension of time is considered, it will be obvious that it takes a finite amount of time for a signal to pass through a gate, and any increase in the number of stages increases the amount of time delay in a system. In some cases this can be an important consideration.

The reader should also clearly understand that the purpose of DeMorganizing is not to simplify logic but to convert from *and-or* logic to *nand* or *nor* logic. However, it is a brute force method. A simpler method derived from this will be shown in Chapter 9.

Too much emphasis need not be put on the subject of simplifying logic for unlike the engineer who is designing circuits to be duplicated in a production run, where the elimination of a single gate can result in the saving of a substantial amount of money, the experimental designer will usually only construct a few pieces of hardware and simplified logic will be more a matter of reliability than monetary savings to him.

If the reader has followed all of the material presented to this point, he will be pleased to know that he has at his command most of the basic concepts of logic design, and what remains to be learned in the later chapters are:

1. labor and error reducing techniques, and
2. how these principles can be applied to solve original apparatus design problems.

By now the following concepts and techniques should be familiar:

1. The standard basis as an orderly means of writing all possible permutations of input states.
2. The designation number (#) as a specification of what the output state will be for each combination of input states listed in the standard basis.
3. A truth table as a specification of all input and output state combinations.
4. The basic functions of *not, or, and, nor,* and *nand,* and the logic flow symbols for these gates.
5. The identities of Boolean algebra and De-Morgan's rules.
6. The general technique of proving two logic statements are equivalent by showing that they have identical designation numbers (or proving they are not equivalent by showing that they have different designation numbers).

7. The notion that identical logic statements have an infinite variety of different forms and that by means of the Boolean identities or some other technique these may be reduced to the simplest possible form to assure reliability and economy in the reduction of logic into hardware.
8. The use of DeMorgan's theorem to convert between *or* and *nand* gates or *and* and *nor* gates.

Chapter 6
Forms of Logic Statements

In the previous chapters it was shown that the first step in logic design is to write a specification or truth table describing what the logic is required to do. Thus, for each possible input permutation in the standard basis it must be decided whether the output (or outputs) will be 1 or 0, and the state column marked accordingly. When this has been done, a unique sequence of 0's and 1's, called a designation number, results which defines the logic needed. There is, however, an infinite set of different logic statements which will produce this effect. It now remains to be shown how to convert a designation number directly into a logic statement. If this can be done, then the entire process of logic design can be reduced to a turn-the-crank kind of operation, and once the truth table is completed in accordance with the design requirements the rest of the job is routine.

To achieve this desirable end, it is necessary to

consider the three basic forms in which logic statements may occur. They are:

1. the sum of products form (SOP)
2. the product of sums form (POS), and
3. the mixed or hybrid form.

The sum of products form is composed of the logical sum of a series of logical products. The following is an example of the sum of products (SOP) form:

$$Z = ABC + A\overline{B}C + AC + B\overline{C}$$

The product of sums form is composed of the logical product of a series of logical sum terms. The following is an example of the product of sums (POS) form:

$$Z = (A + B + C) \cdot (A + \overline{B} + C) \cdot (A + C) \cdot (B + \overline{C})$$

The hybrid or mixed form simply contains both types of terms. Examples of a mixed form would be:

$$Z = A(B + C) + CD$$
$$Z = [A + (B \cdot C)] \cdot (CD)$$

Any logical statement can also be expressed in either of two general forms, called canonical forms.

The first canonical form is a special type of sum of products form. It is the sum of a set of elementary products. An elementary product is one that contains each input variable or its negation once and only once. Thus for a three input system the following are each elementary products:

$$ABC$$
$$A\overline{B}C$$
$$AB\overline{C}$$
etc.

The following do not meet the definition of an elementary product:

AC one term missing
$AC\overline{A}B$ one term appears twice

Table 6–1 shows all of the elementary products possible for a three input variable system together with their designation numbers. These elementary products are called minterms and are abbreviated by a lower case m and subscript as shown.

Table 6–1

State	0	1	2	3	4	5	6	7
A	0	1	0	1	0	1	0	1
B	0	0	1	1	0	0	1	1
C	0	0	0	0	1	1	1	1
$\overline{A}$	1	0	1	0	1	0	1	0
$\overline{B}$	1	1	0	0	1	1	0	0
$\overline{C}$	1	1	1	1	0	0	0	0

Minterm (or Elementary Product)		Designation Numbers							
m_0	$\overline{A} \cdot \overline{B} \cdot \overline{C}$	1	0	0	0	0	0	0	0
m_1	$A \cdot \overline{B} \cdot \overline{C}$	0	1	0	0	0	0	0	0
m_2	$\overline{A} \cdot B \cdot \overline{C}$	0	0	1	0	0	0	0	0
m_3	$A \cdot B \cdot \overline{C}$	0	0	0	1	0	0	0	0
m_4	$\overline{A} \cdot \overline{B} \cdot C$	0	0	0	0	1	0	0	0
m_5	$A \cdot \overline{B} \cdot C$	0	0	0	0	0	1	0	0
m_6	$\overline{A} \cdot B \cdot C$	0	0	0	0	0	0	1	0
m_7	$A \cdot B \cdot C$	0	0	0	0	0	0	0	1

From Table 6–1 it can be seen that there are eight different elementary products in a three variable system. It can also be seen that the designation number for each elementary product or minterm is a single 1 in a set of 0's. Thus, each state position or bit (short for binary digit) in a designation number having a value of 1 stands for a minterm.

To write a logical statement in the first canonical form, simply write a logical sum of all of the minterms represented as follows:

	m_0	m_1	m_2	m_3	m_4	m_5	m_6	m_7
Given: #	0	0	1	1	0	0	1	1

$$\text{Then:} \quad Z = m_2 + m_3 + m_6 + m_7$$
$$= \overline{A}B\overline{C} + AB\overline{C} + \overline{A}BC + ABC$$

Figure 6–1 shows the logic diagram that represents this function and also shows why the sum of products form is often called the *and*-to-*or* logic form.

The observant reader will have noticed that the designation number of this function is the same as that for the second input variable, B. Hence the entire logic diagram of Figure 6–1 can be reduced to a permanent wire connected to input B. This demonstrates that the use of minterms does not produce the simplest possible logical statement. Their advantage lies in that they allow the designer to write a logic statement and diagram directly from a designation number (which is a statement of the system specifications).

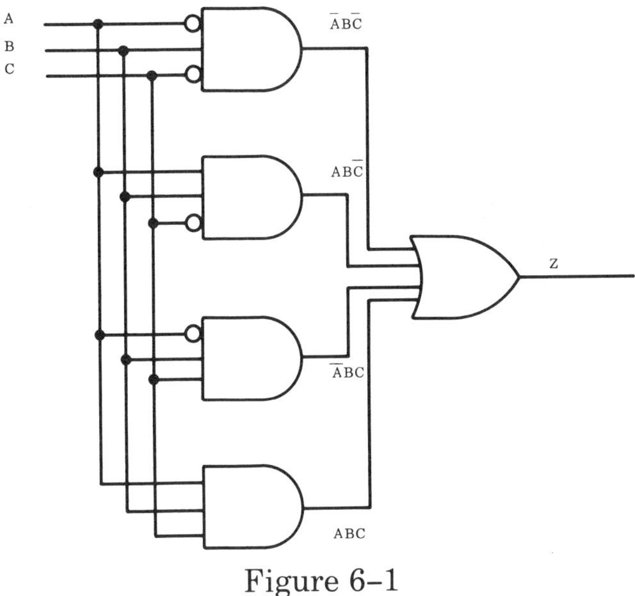

Figure 6-1

Figure 6-1 discloses still another way of simplifying logic, namely the careful study of logic
diagrams. A careful look at this diagram reveals
that the variable *B* appears *or*ed with all possible
combinations of *A*, *C*, and their negation. Hence, *B*
is the only relevant requirement for a 1 output of
the system.

About the only problem involved in the use of
minterms is remembering which of the eight possible elementary products corresponds to a particu-

lar minterm. This can be done by reference to the foregoing table, but in the event that such a table is not available there is a very useful technique, which will find many other applications in the area of logic design, namely the assigning of weights or values to the variables. Thus,

$$\text{Let:} \quad A = 1 \quad B = 2 \quad C = 4$$
$$\text{Then:} \quad \overline{A} = 0 \quad \overline{B} = 0 \quad \overline{C} = 0$$

in other words when one of the three variables is in the 1 state, it has the value assigned, and when it is in the 0 state it has no value. The elementary product $\overline{A}BC$, thus, has an assigned value of 0 plus 2 plus 4 which equals 6. Therefore $\overline{A}BC = m_6$. The value of each minterm in accordance with this scheme will be equal to its subscript number.

The second canonical form is a special product of sums form. It is the product of a set of elementary sums. An elementary sum is one in which each variable or its negation appears once and only once. As in the case of elementary products, there are 2^N possible elementary sums in a system of N input variables. An elementary sum is called a maxterm and is designated by an upper case M with a subscript. The following are examples of maxterms in a three input system:

$$A + B + C$$
$$A + \overline{B} + C$$
$$A + B + \overline{C}$$
$$\text{etc.}$$

The following do not meet the definition of an elementary sum:

$$A + C \qquad \text{one term missing}$$
$$A + C + \overline{A} + B \quad \text{one term appears twice}$$

Table 6–2 shows all of the elementary sums for a three input system together with their designation numbers.

Table 6–2

State	0	1	2	3	4	5	6	7
A	0	1	0	1	0	1	0	1
B	0	0	1	1	0	0	1	1
C	0	0	0	0	1	1	1	1
$\overline{A}$	1	0	1	0	1	0	1	0
$\overline{B}$	1	1	0	0	1	1	0	0
$\overline{C}$	1	1	1	1	0	0	0	0

Maxterm (or Elementary sum)		Designation Numbers						
M_0	$A + B + C$	0	1	1	1	1	1	1	1
M_1	$\overline{A} + B + C$	1	0	1	1	1	1	1	1
M_2	$A + \overline{B} + C$	1	1	0	1	1	1	1	1
M_3	$\overline{A} + \overline{B} + C$	1	1	1	0	1	1	1	1
M_4	$A + B + \overline{C}$	1	1	1	1	0	1	1	1
M_5	$\overline{A} + B + \overline{C}$	1	1	1	1	1	0	1	1
M_6	$A + \overline{B} + \overline{C}$	1	1	1	1	1	1	0	1
M_7	$\overline{A} + \overline{B} + \overline{C}$	1	1	1	1	1	1	1	0

From Table 6–2 it will be obvious that each maxterm is the complement or negation of the corresponding minterm; i.e., the 0's and 1's in the designation numbers are reversed. Thus:

$$m_1 = \overline{M_1}$$
$$\text{or } A \cdot \overline{B} \cdot \overline{C} = \overline{\overline{A} + B + C}$$

To write a logic statement directly in the second canonical form, simply let each state position or bit stand for a maxterm and write the product of those maxterms having a 0 under them in the designation number as follows:

	M_0	M_1	M_2	M_3	M_4	M_5	M_6	M_7
Given: #	0	0	1	1	0	0	1	1
Then: $Z =$	$M_0 \cdot$		$M_1 \cdot$		$M_4 \cdot$		M_5	

$$= (A + B + C) \cdot (\overline{A} + B + C) \cdot (A + B + \overline{C}) \cdot (\overline{A} + B + \overline{C})$$

Figure 6–2 shows the implementation of this logic statement in a logic diagram and also shows why the product of sums form is often referred to as *or*-to-*and* logic.

Again the only difficulty involved is in remembering which elementary sum corresponds to each maxterm. This can be done in exactly the same way that minterms were remembered. Now however, since maxterms are represented in designation numbers by the presence of a 0 instead of a 1, the following weighting system is used:

$$\text{Let: } \quad \overline{A} = 1 \quad \overline{B} = 2 \quad \overline{C} = 4$$
$$\text{Then: } \quad A = 0 \quad B = 0 \quad C = 0$$

In general the *and*-to-*or* logic (SOP) and the

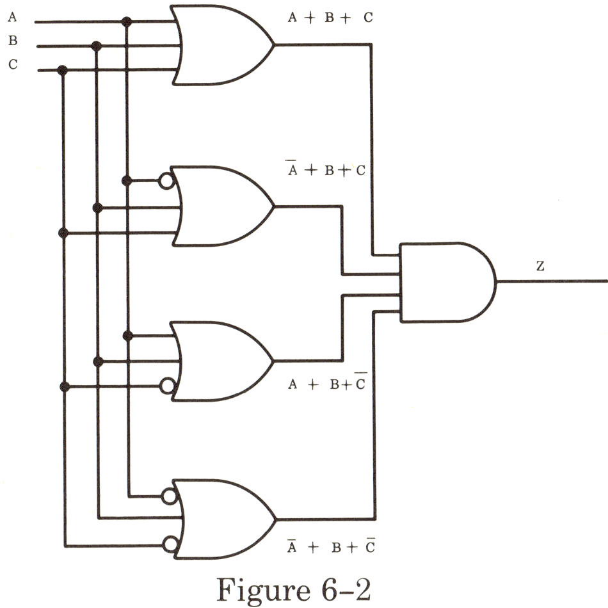

Figure 6–2

or-to-*and* logic (POS) will yield a different number of gates and stages, and in some cases one method will be simpler than the other, but neither generally yields the simplest possible form of a logic statement. The choice of which type of logic to use will be governed by the type of commercial gates it is ultimately desired to use. *And*-to-*or* logic converts readily into nand logic by DeMorgan's theorems, while *or*-to-*and* logic converts readily into nor gate logic.

Chapter 7
Binary Numbers and Arithmetic

In all of the preceding chapters on logic design, the binary states of 0 and 1 referred to either logic states or, in an apparatus setting, the two possible conditions or states of a piece of equipment. It is possible and useful, however, to use the same types of basic gates discussed in a setting where the 0's and 1's represent numerical quantities. The distinction between these numbers standing for logical versus numerical quantities must always be kept clearly in mind, for often in a single system both logical and numerical quantities may be involved in different components of the overall system. It is the purpose of this chapter to introduce the reader to the basic concepts involved in digital or, more properly, binary arithmetic. The very first concept that must be examined is the idea of a number system.

Most people are familiar with the decimal system of numbers that they have been using all of their lives. It is sometimes hard to realize that this familiar system is completely arbitrary.

The decimal system uses ten symbols to represent things counted. They are the following: 0, 1, 2, 3, 4, 5, 6, 7, 8, and 9. Consider the following decimal number:

$$235$$

The extreme right-hand position represents the number of things counted. After counting nine items, there are no symbols left so what is done is to carry a 1 over to the next column to the left and start over counting in the extreme right column. When the middle column reaches number 9, the symbols are again exhausted so a 1 is carried over to the third column and the counting is continued, and so on. Thus, the extreme right-hand position represents units or individual things counted. The next column to the left represents tens of things counted (since it takes nine items to fill the first position), the third position represents hundreds of things counted, and so on in steps of powers of 10. Therefore, the number 456235 means:

5 units + 3 tens + 2 hundreds + 6 thousands
+ 5 ten thousands + 4 hundred thousands

This in turn could be written as:

$$5 + 30 + 200 + 6000 + 50,000 + 400,000$$

But:

$$
\begin{array}{lll}
1 = 10^0 & 100 = 10^2 & 10,000 = 10^4 \\
10 = 10^1 & 1000 = 10^3 & 100,000 = 10^5
\end{array}
$$

Therefore, the original decimal number may be re-written in the following convenient powers of ten notation:

$$5 \times 10^0$$
$$+ 3 \times 10^1$$
$$+ 2 \times 10^2$$
$$+ 6 \times 10^3$$
$$+ 5 \times 10^4$$
$$+ 4 \times 10^5$$

This notation clearly shows the meaning of each digit in the original number, 456235. The reason that powers of ten are involved in this number system is not due to the magic of the number ten (even though mental multiplication and division of decimal numbers by powers of ten is accomplished by simply moving a decimal point), but because there are ten symbols in our decimal number system. The number of symbols in a number system is called its modulus.

The powers of ten notation can, of course, be used for digits on the right of the decimal point by an extension of the foregoing matrix. For example, 25.328 means:

$$8 \times 10^{-3}$$
$$+ 2 \times 10^{-2}$$
$$+ 3 \times 10^{-1}$$
$$+ 5 \times 10^0$$
$$+ 2 \times 10^1$$

It is assumed that the reader is familiar with the fact that:

$$10^{-1} = \frac{1}{10} = 0.1$$

$$10^{-2} = \frac{1}{10^2} = \frac{1}{100} = 0.01$$

etc.

The reader should notice that in the foregoing the $+$ sign is being used to indicate arithmetic addition — not logical addition or the *or* function.

A number system can be based on any number of basic symbols. For example, a system having a modulus of 4 would utilize only the following symbols: 0, 1, 2, and 3. A system with a modulus of 12 might use the following symbols: 0, 1, 2, 3, 4, 5, 6, 7, 8, 9, \$, and ¢.

Let us consider a system of only 4 symbols, 0, 1, 2, and 3. In such a system the number 231 would represent:

$$1 \text{ unit} + 3 \times (4) + 2 \times (4 \times 4)$$

Or:

$$\begin{aligned} & 1 \times 4^0 \\ + & 3 \times 4^1 \\ + & 2 \times 4^2 \end{aligned}$$

Thus in a modulus 4 number system, each position in a number now represents some power of 4 as opposed to a power of 10 in the decimal system. It is a general rule that each position in a number written in a modulus N system of numbers will represent some power of N increasing successively from right to left. (As a matter of convention, the least significant symbol is the one on the extreme right.)

The system of numbers that is of most interest to logic designers has a modulus of 2 and utilizes only two symbols, 1 and 0. This is called the binary system, and each symbol position in the number is called a bit, which is short for "binary digit." In accordance with the foregoing material, the binary number 101001 represents the following:

$$
\begin{aligned}
1 \times 2^0 &= 1 \times 1 = 1 \\
+\, 0 \times 2^1 &= 0 \times 2 = 0 \\
+\, 0 \times 2^2 &= 0 \times 4 = 0 \\
+\, 1 \times 2^3 &= 1 \times 8 = 8 \\
+\, 0 \times 2^4 &= 0 \times 16 = 0 \\
+\, 1 \times 2^5 &= 1 \times 32 = \underline{32} \\
& 41
\end{aligned}
$$

This shows that each position in a binary number represents some power of two. It also illustrates a general method of converting a binary to a decimal number: simply multiply each 1 in the binary number by the appropriate power of two and add to get the decimal number. Thus, the binary number $101001 = 41$ in the decimal system.

Table 7–1 shows the first 20 binary numbers in a matrix format.

Normally, nonsignificant 0's, i.e., those to the left of the last 1, are not written (as is the case in

Table 7–1

Decimal Number	Bit	Binary Number							
		2^7 128	2^6 64	2^5 32	2^4 16	2^3 8	2^2 4	2^1 2	2^0 1
0		0	0	0	0	0	0	0	0
1		0	0	0	0	0	0	0	1
2		0	0	0	0	0	0	1	0
3		0	0	0	0	0	0	1	1
4		0	0	0	0	0	1	0	0
5		0	0	0	0	0	1	0	1
6		0	0	0	0	0	1	1	0
7		0	0	0	0	0	1	1	1
8		0	0	0	0	1	0	0	0
9		0	0	0	0	1	0	0	1
10		0	0	0	0	1	0	1	0
11		0	0	0	0	1	0	1	1
12		0	0	0	0	1	1	0	0
13		0	0	0	0	1	1	0	1
14		0	0	0	0	1	1	1	0
15		0	0	0	0	1	1	1	1
16		0	0	0	1	0	0	0	0
17		0	0	0	1	0	0	0	1
18		0	0	0	1	0	0	1	0
19		0	0	0	1	0	0	1	1
20		0	0	0	1	0	1	0	0

the decimal system). The reader should note how the numbers change as counting proceeds and should learn the first ten or so by rote.

The general method of generating a binary number from a decimal number will now be described. Simply pick the bit position corresponding to the highest power of two that will fit into the decimal number and mark a 1 for that bit. Then subtract the decimal quantity that this bit represents from the original decimal number and do the same for the difference until the difference is 0. For example, to convert 35 into a binary number:

$$
\begin{aligned}
&\text{Powers of 2}\\
2^0 &= 1\\
2^1 &= 2\\
2^2 &= 4\\
2^3 &= 8\\
2^4 &= 16\\
2^5 &= 32\\
2^6 &= 64 \quad \text{(Stop writing here since}\\
&\qquad\qquad 64 \text{ is greater than 35 and}\\
&\qquad\qquad \text{thus can't be fitted into}\\
&\qquad\qquad \text{it.)}
\end{aligned}
$$

The largest power of 2 that goes into 35 is 32 so the bit representing 32 is assigned a 1 and becomes the most significant bit in the binary number:

32	16	8	4	2	1
1					

$$35 - 32 = 3$$

The next largest valued bit that fits into 3 is the position representing 2; hence we write:

32	16	8	4	2	1
1	0	0	0	1	

$$3 - 2 = 1$$

But the next bit position has a value exactly equal to 1; hence the complete binary number can be written as:

32	16	8	4	2	1
1	0	0	0	1	1

It will be noticed that this number was written directly without having to count up to it.

Once the designer is familiar with the notation in the binary system, he will discover that all of the rules of arithmetic that he is familiar with under the decimal system still apply. Basically there is only one operation in arithmetic, namely addition. Thus when it is said that $3 + 2 = 5$, this is in effect saying that if a stick of 3 units is placed at the end of a stick of 2 units the overall dimension of the two sticks combined would be 5 units. In the case of saying $5 - 3 = 2$, this means that if a 5 unit stick is partly covered with a 3 unit stick the uncovered portion will be 2 units. Thus, subtraction is basically addition with signed numbers.

The expression 3×4 means to add 3 four times or to add 4 three times. Hence multiplication reduces to successive addition. Division is merely the inverse process, and hence it may also be resolved into addition, as can successive multiplication of a number by itself (raising to a power) or the inverse process of extracting a root.

As has been shown, the basic operation of addition is simply a counting process. As each digit position in the number system used is filled up, a unit carry is moved to the next higher position. The only difference between the decimal system and the binary system with respect to this carry procedure is that each digit position in the decimal system has a symbol capacity of 10 while in the binary system the symbol capacity is only 2. Thus the two basic steps involved in addition are counting within a digit position and a carry over to the next highest position. Binary numbers are useful because they permit the use of two state systems in addition and all the other more complex types of arithmetic operations.

Chapter 8
Positive and Negative Logic

It is not the intention of this book to go into any detail regarding the design of the circuits used in the basic logic gates, because they are commercially available in the form of subminiature, economical, integrated circuit packages and are not customarily built up from discrete components. The logic designer will, therefore, never actually build the basic circuits used. Nevertheless, it will be instructive to look at some of the devices that theoretically could be used.

It has already been shown how switches and relays can be used to make *and* or *or* gates. Let us now consider how diodes could be used to produce these functions.

A diode is a device that has a high degree of resistance to the passage of an electric current in one direction and a low degree of resistance to the passage of a current in the opposite direction. As shown in Figure 8–1, it is usually a cylindrical device about the size of a $\frac{1}{2}$ watt resistor and is symbolized by a line and an arrowhead. The arrowhead points in the direction in which a positive voltage produces an unimpeded current flow. The resistance in this direction, or the forward resistance, is usually less than 20 ohms. The resistance in the other direction, or the back resistance, is usually greater than 20,000 ohms.

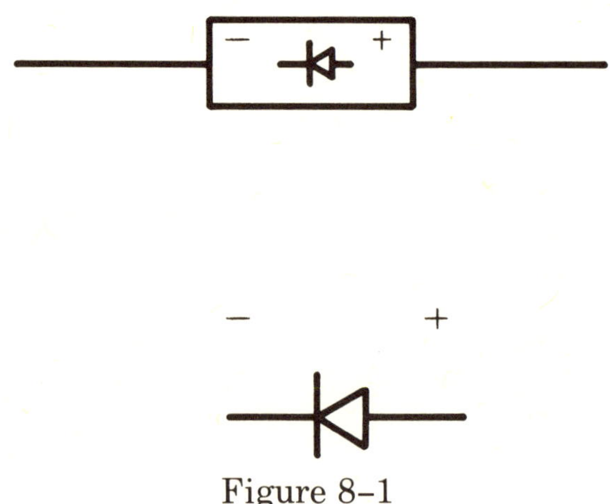

Figure 8–1

The peak inverse voltage rating of a diode is the greatest amount of voltage that can be applied to the device in the nonconducting or reverse direction before it breaks down. This figure should be at least several times greater than the inverse voltage that the device is ever exposed to in an actual circuit.

Figure 8–2 shows three diodes and a resistor connected to form a gate.

$$\text{If } 1 = +28 \text{ V}$$
$$\text{and } 0 = 0 \text{ V}$$

then the circuit of Figure 8–2 is an *and* gate. The only time the output, Z, can be 1 (+28 V) is when all three input lines have 1's (+28 V) on them, since the presence of a single 0 (0 V) will cause its diode to conduct and act like a short circuit, or wire connected across the remaining diodes, putting 0 volts on the output. Thus the circuit could be represented on a logic diagram as an *and* gate, and the general function symbol shown in dotted lines could be replaced by an *and* gate symbol.

On the other hand,

$$\text{if } 1 = 0 \text{ V}$$
$$\text{and } 0 = +28 \text{ V}$$

then the identical circuit will now function as an *or* gate, since now only one of the input lines needs to be 1 (0 V) to get a 1 (0 V) output of Z.

The difference between an *and* and an *or* gate in this situation is determined not by the hardware but by how the two logic states, 0 and 1, are arbitrarily defined.

As a matter of definition, when a logical 1 and 0 are represented in a system by different voltage levels, if the 1 is represented by the more positive voltage the logic is called *positive logic,* and if the 1 is represented by the more negative voltage the logic

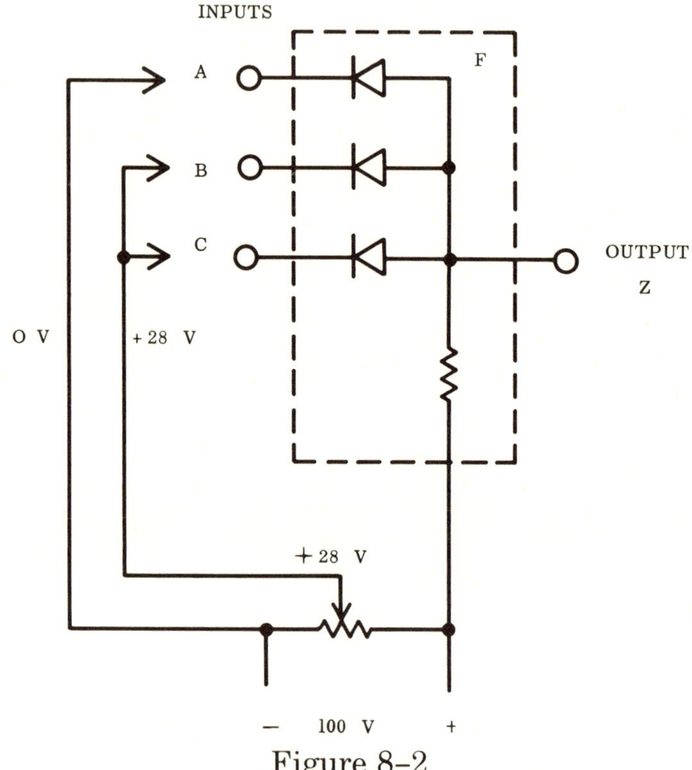

Figure 8–2

is called *negative logic*. The following shows how the same pairs of voltage levels can be used in either positive or negative logic systems:

Positive Logic		Negative Logic	
1	0	1	0
+28 V	0 V	0 V	+28 V
+5 V	0 V	0 V	+5 V
0 V	−5 V	−5 V	0 V
+15 V	+5 V	+5 V	+15 V
−5 V	−15 V	−15 V	−5 V
etc.			

It should be apparent that in the circuit of Figure 8–2 the polarity of the power supply alone does not determine the kind of gate that the circuit forms, since if both the power supply polarity and the diodes were reversed the device would still be an *and* gate with positive logic and an *or* gate with negative logic. These functions are strictly determined by the definition of the 1 and 0 levels and not the hardware. Thus, the designer has a completely arbitrary choice of which type of logic to use. This is also true in the more common case where transistors or micrologic are used to produce gates. Here the power supply polarity cannot be changed, for these devices require a definite polarity, but the designer can still use either positive or negative logic depending on how he choses to define his 0 and 1 states.

This means in effect that every time a gate is

purchased two different gates are obtained for the same money depending on how the designer chooses to use it.

The potential for two different functions to be performed by the same piece of hardware is what is meant by the concept of duality, and the *and* gate is said to be the dual of the *or* gate.

The dual of a function, F, is designated by $d(F)$.

The basic duals that the reader should become familiar with are:

F	Dual of F
and	or
nand	nor
1	0
A	A
not	not

The foregoing table is reversible. Thus if *and* is the dual of *or*, then *or* is also the dual of *and*. It can be seen that the *not* function or any of the input variables have no true duals; i.e., their function is independent of whether positive or negative logic is used.

To find the dual of a complex function it is necessary to replace each basic function or each term with its dual; e.g.,

$$F = \overline{A}BC + A\overline{D}E + BD\overline{C} \qquad \text{SOP form}$$
$$d(F) = (\overline{A} + B + C) \cdot (A + \overline{D} + E) \qquad \text{POS form}$$
$$\cdot (B + D + \overline{C})$$

From the foregoing it will be realized that the

first and second canonical forms are in fact the duals of each other. Therefore any logic statement can be implemented in the *and*-to-*or* form or the *or*-to-*and* form using the identical type of hardware depending on whether positive or negative logic is decided upon.

It should be obvious that a dual does not have the same designation number as the function from which it was derived for they are not the same function. A dual is obtained as a result of the same hardware performing a different function.

To find the designation number of a dual from the designation number of the original function:

1. Write the original designation number backwards.
2. Invert each bit; i.e., write the complement of this backwards designation number.

Example 1:	$\#F =$		0	0	0	1	(the *and* function)
	(1)	1	0	0	0	
$d(F)$	(2)	0	1	1	1	(the *or* function)
Example 2:	$\#F =$		0	1	0	1	(A)
	(1)	1	0	1	0	
$d(F)$	(2)	0	1	0	1	(Still A. This is why $d(A) = A$.)

The concept of duality is vastly more important to the experimental equipment designer than to the logic engineer who is designing a production run of commercial equipment. The design engineer will:

1. Decide what set of commercial logic packages he will use.
2. Decide whether to use positive or negative logic based on economy in accomplishing his design goals.

The experimental equipment designer on the other hand will rarely want to build a hard wired package. It is more appropriate for his purposes to connect his basic modules to some form of patching panel so that he can conveniently change his system configurations and hence use the same basic modules in a variety of different applications at different times. For him the concept of duality will result in the effective doubling of his research equipment budget.

Chapter 9
Logic Simplification

The reader has already learned that there are an infinite number of ways that a given logic function can be implemented. Thus there are an infinite number of equivalent logic statements.

It has been shown in chapter six how to write the logic statement for any designation number directly from this number in terms of a canonical SOP or POS form. In general these forms of logic statements will not be the simplest possible and must be further simplified. They are merely starting points in design. The designer is faced with the dual problem of:

1. Simplifying these basic statements, and
2. Determining when he has the simplest possible expression for the required function.

While there are techniques available to provide an answer to the latter question, the experimental equipment designer will rarely be involved with systems so complex that he will have to concern himself with the question of whether what appears to be a good way of solving his particular problem is really the simplest possible way. Also, the latter question may have no answer because the reduction of the number of gates in a system may have to be accomplished by increasing the number of stages and, hence, the delay time. Thus, the final choice of design may have to be the result of a trade off between several desirable but mutually exclusive goals. As a practical working standard for prototype or non-production designs, the design will be assumed to be simple enough if there are no obvious simplifications possible using the techniques to be discussed in this chapter. To a considerable extent the simplicity of the final designs will be a function of the skill of the designer, and with experience he will tend to produce simpler, and therefore better, systems.

As in the case of experimental designs the simpler the design of equipment the better, but for different reasons. In the design of an experiment, the simpler the design the easier it is both to run it and to determine precisely what the results indicate. In the case of equipment design, the simpler design requires fewer component parts. The smaller the number of required components the greater the economy, reliability, and maintainability of the system. In the design of experimental apparatus, comparatively small monetary savings will result from the elimination of a few components, but there will be big dividends just the same. There will be fewer parts to fail. Also a simpler system makes it easier for a person with less experience in equipment design to go about troubleshooting if the system fails. Lastly, a simpler system is quicker to assemble and check out (or debug).

There are several techniques which can be used to simplify logic, some of which have already been discussed. While they will be dealt with separately, with experience the logic designer will learn how to use several techniques together when necessary. He will also learn which technique is the most useful for a given problem, just as a plumber learns which tool is best for a specific job.

BOOLEAN ALGEBRA

The most basic method of logic simplification is by applying the identities of Boolean algebra to simplify statements and replace complex or redundant forms with simpler ones. Facility in the use of this technique, as with ordinary algebra, comes mainly from practice and familiarity with the basic identities. For example, anytime that the same variable appears in a gate with its negation it is obvious that the variable is irrelevant and the entire gate may be eliminated; e.g.:

1. $AB\overline{A} = 0$ (because $A \cdot \overline{A} = 0$)

   In other words since A and $\overline{A}$ can never both be 1 at the same time, the foregoing *and* gate can never have an output of 1; hence it can be replaced with a permanently wired 0 level signal.

2. $A + B + \overline{A} = 1$ (because $A + \overline{A} = 1$)

Since whatever state A is in there will always be a 1 level signal going into the *or* gate, the output of this gate will always be at the 1 level. Thus the gate can be replaced with a permanent wire to a constant 1 level signal.

The foregoing also holds true for *and* and *or* gates with more than three inputs.

ALTERNATE DESIGNS

Since it is so easy to write a logic statement directly from a designation number in terms of minterms (*and*-to-*or* logic) or maxterms (*or*-to-*and* logic), both forms should be written and the simpler chosen. But actually it is not even necessary to bother to write out these forms. Since there is one minterm in the sum of products form for each 1 in the designation number and one maxterm in the product of sums form for each 0 in the designation number, it is clear that if the designation number is composed mainly of 0's minterms will yield the simpler result, while a designation number composed mainly of 1's should be treated with maxterms.

STUDY OF LOGIC DIAGRAMS

A very useful technique for simplifying designs is to draw a logic diagram directly and label all of the intermediate functions (i.e., the output of each gate in the system). Then look for redundant gates and functions. If the logic statement is written directly in the SOP or POS form, there will be no redundant gates if only one output variable is involved, but it is often the case in practical systems that several output variables will be needed. In this case several identical gates may be called for in the logic statements, and these need appear only once in the hardware. For example, consider the system of Figure 9–1. Here there are three input signals, A, B, and C, and two output variables, F_1 and F_2.

$$F_1 = \#\quad 0\quad 1\quad 1\quad 0\quad 0\quad 1\quad 0\quad 0$$
$$= A \cdot \overline{B} \cdot \overline{C} \ + \ \overline{A} \cdot B \cdot \overline{C} \ + \ A \cdot \overline{B} \cdot C \text{ (SOP form}$$

from minterms)

(Note there are 8 bits in the designation number because there are 3 input variables. With 4, there would be 16 bits, etc.)

$$F_2 = \#\quad 0\quad 0\quad 1\quad 0\quad 1\quad 1\quad 0\quad 0$$
$$= \overline{A} \cdot B \cdot \overline{C} \ + \ \overline{A} \cdot \overline{B} \cdot C \ + \ A \cdot \overline{B} \cdot C \text{ (SOP form)}$$

A study of Figure 9–1 shows:

1. There are really only four *and* gates required since gates 2 and 4 are identical in function — as are gates 3 and 6. Since the output of these gates is the same, only one gate need be used in each case.
2. There are only three input variables or their negation; hence they can be taken from the three basic signal lines and negated as required.

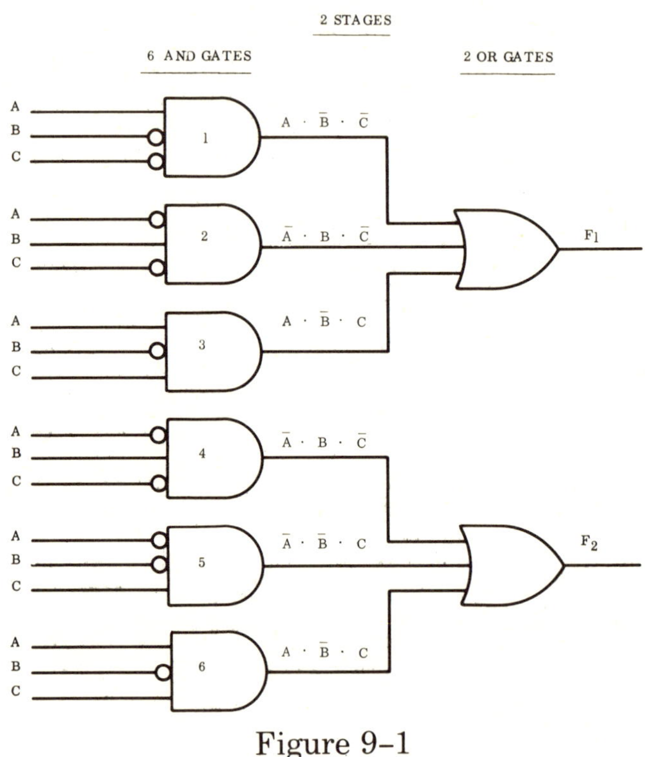

Figure 9–1

Figure 9–2 incorporates these two simplifications.

It would be convenient if the logic diagram could be converted into nand logic directly by graphical means without having to resort to the cumbersome manipulations of DeMorgan's theorems. This can be done by remembering the familiar English principle that a double negative amounts to an affirmative. Thus, if a negation symbol were added to the output of each *and* gate, a nand gate would result. If a negation symbol were then added to these same lines when they get to the input of the *or* gate, the logic would not have been affected at all. However, all of the inputs to the *or* gates will now be negated. But by DeMorgan's theorem for a three variable system: $\overline{A} + \overline{B} + \overline{C} = \overline{ABC}$. Therefore, the modified *or* gate is now equivalent to a nand gate, and the system has been completely transformed from an *and*-to-*or* system to a nand system. Figure 9–3 demonstrates these two steps with a simpler system for the sake of clarity.

If the original logic had been in the *or*-to-*and* form (i.e., written from maxterms instead of minterms), the foregoing procedures would have resulted in nor instead of nand logic, as shown in Figure 9–4.

For practice the reader could show that the alternate expressions for the output functions in Figure 9–3(c) and Figure 9–4(c) are equivalent by DeMorgan's theorems. However, if the bracketed terms are treated as single variables, it will be apparent by inspection that these forms reduce to DeMorgan's two identities.

Matrix Method

Figure 9–5 shows a matrix drawn for a three input variable system with four output variables.

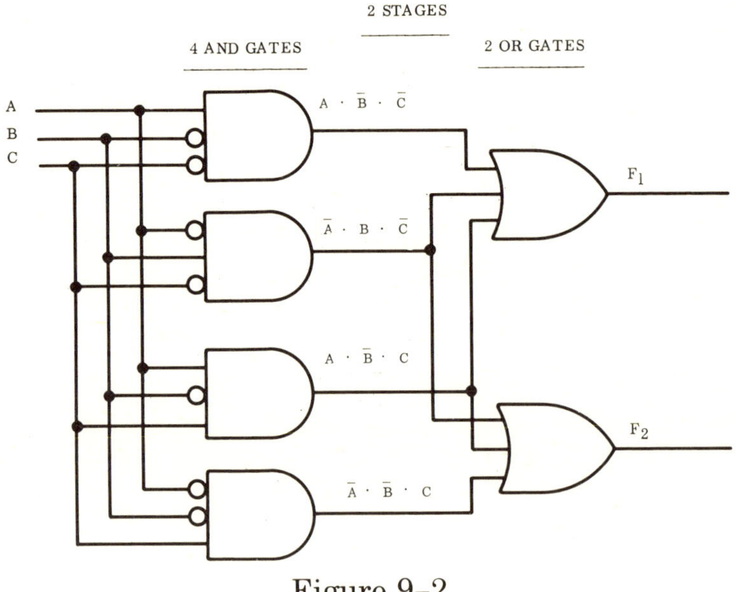

Figure 9–2

A   ORIGINAL AND—TO—OR LOGIC
A
B
C
ABC
ABC
D
E
DE
DE
F = ABC + DE

B   EQUIVALANT DOUBLE NEGATED LOGIC
A
B
C
ABC
ABC
D
E
DE
DE
F = ABC + DE

C   EQUIVALENT NAND LOGIC
A
B
C
ABC
ABC
D
E
DE
DE
F = (ABC) · (DE)
= ABC + DE

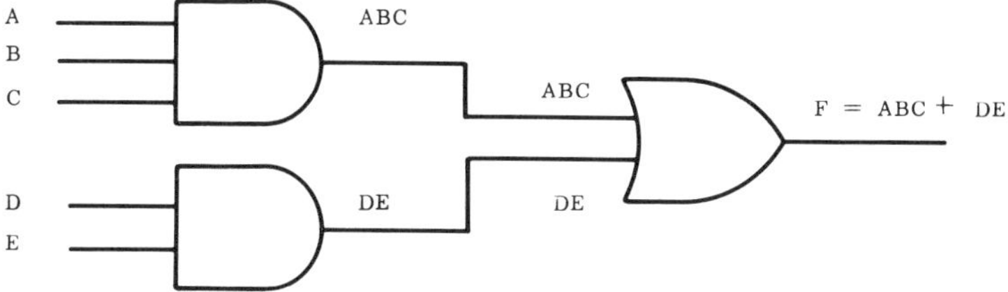

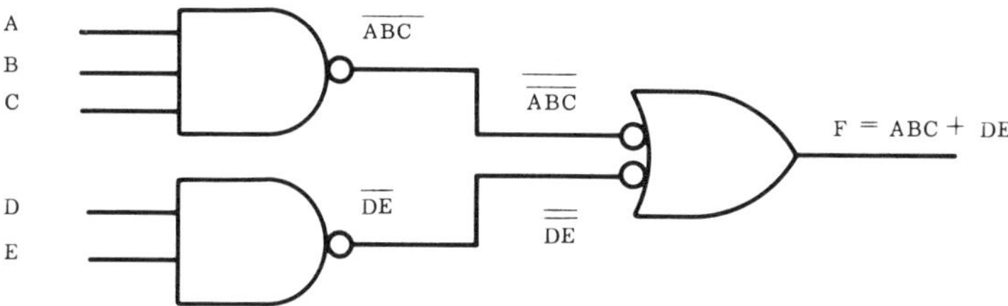

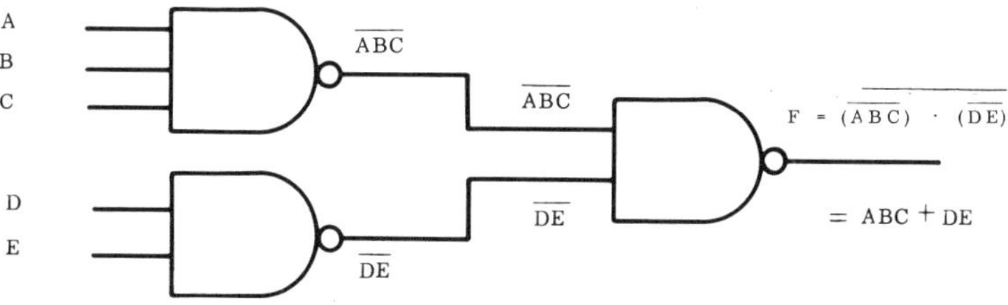

Figure 9-3

A   ORIGINAL OR-TO-AND LOGIC
A
B
C
D
E
A + B + C
A + B + C
D + E
D + E
F = (A+B+C) · (D+E)

B   EQUIVALENT DOUBLE NEGATED LOGIC
A
B
C
D
E
$\overline{A+B+C}$
$\overline{\overline{A+B+C}}$
$\overline{\overline{D+E}}$
$\overline{D+E}$
F = (A+B+C) · (D+E)

C   EQUIVALENT NOR LOGIC
A
B
C
D
E
$\overline{A+B+C}$
$\overline{A+B+C}$
$\overline{D+E}$
$\overline{D+E}$
F = $\overline{\overline{(A+B+C)}+\overline{(D+E)}}$
= (A+B+C) (D+E)

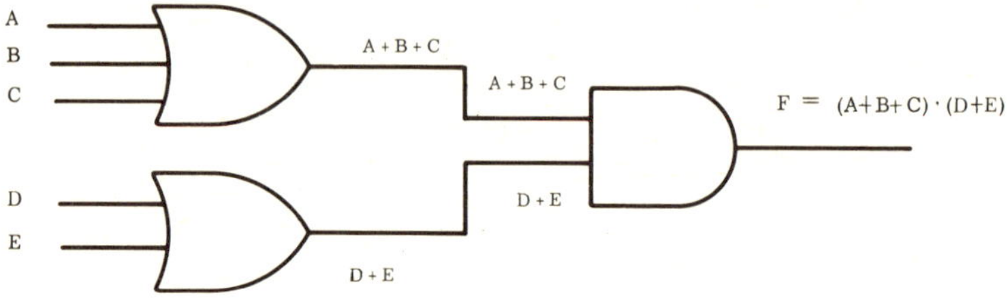

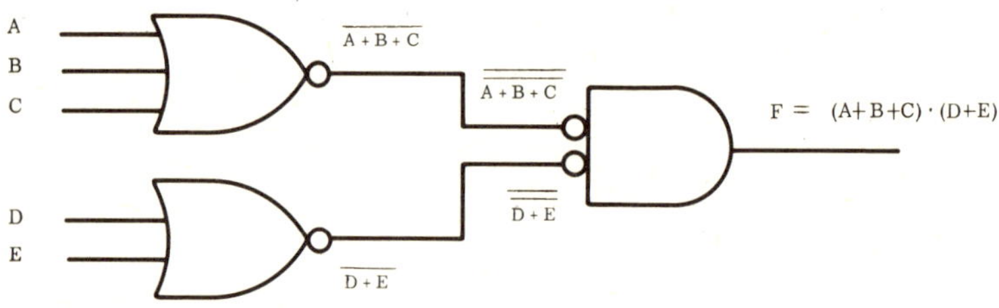

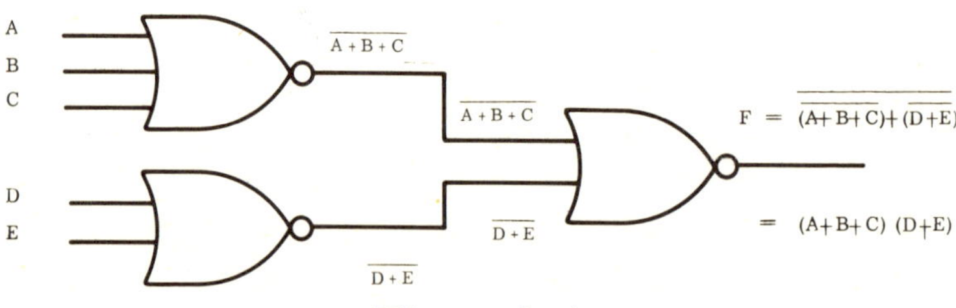

Figure 9-4

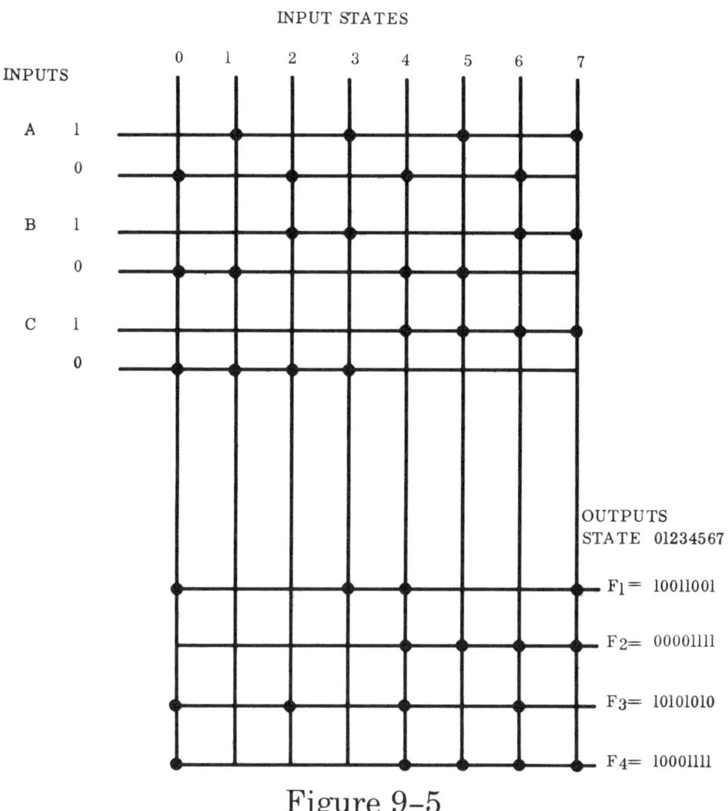

Figure 9–5

A study of this figure discloses that the matrix shown is a direct way of designing a logical system. It should be noticed that the upper portion of the matrix is just another way of writing a standard basis. For each input variable there are two horizontal lines, one for a 1 level and one for a 0 level. If the variable is taken as having a 1 value in a particular state, a dot is drawn at the intersection of the vertical line representing the state and the horizontal 1 line for that variable. If the variable is taken as 0 in a state, the dot is drawn on the 0 line. Thus the 1 line for variable A represents A, and the 0 line represents $\overline{A}$.

Not only does the upper part of the matrix represent the standard basis, but it will be further noted that the three dots under the vertical line representing each input state position represent the minterm corresponding to this state. For example, the dots under state 0 are equivalent to $\overline{A} \cdot \overline{B} \cdot \overline{C}$, which equals m_0. Thus the vertical lines in the matrix represent *and* gates, and the functions *and*ed in each state make up the appropriate minterm.

At the bottom of the matrix there are horizontal lines, one for each output function. It will be noted that, for each 1 in the designation number defining the output function, a dot is drawn on the intersection of the vertical line representing the corresponding input state and the horizontal line representing the function. Thus the horizontal function lines represent *or* gates, and the dots indicate which of the minterm *and* gates are fed into these *or* gates.

Therefore, it can be appreciated that the matrix cf Figure 9–5 makes it possible to write a logic diagram directly in *and*-to-*or* logic form. It should also be clear that this matrix can be used with any number of input and output variables with equal facility.

Having obtained a canonical form of logic from

the matrix, the next step is to use the matrix to simplify the logic.

Figure 9–6 shows the first simplifications that can be made by inspection. It is obvious that the designation number for F_3 is the same as for $\overline{A}$. Therefore, this *or* gate can be eliminated and replaced with a simple *not* function or inverter. (One

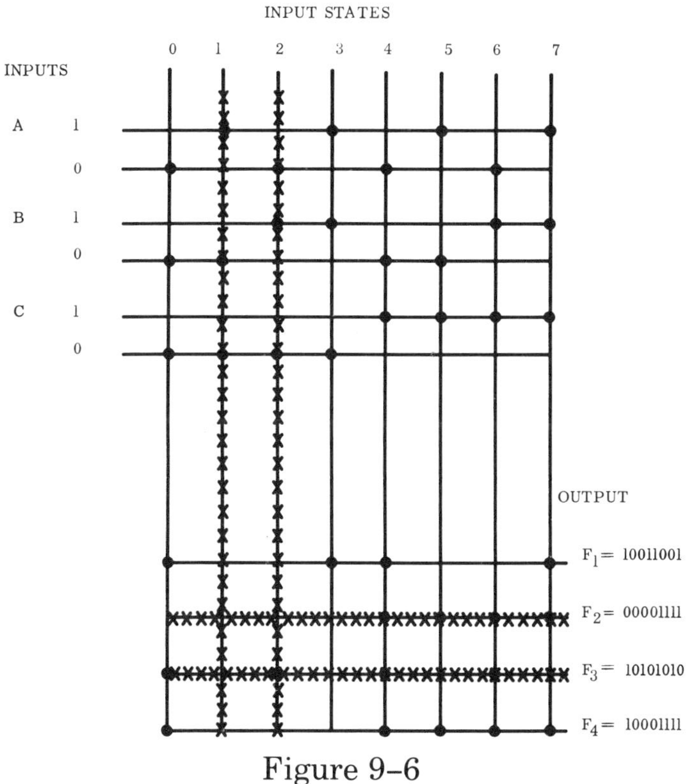

Figure 9–6

common way of providing a *not* function is to use a nor gate with only one input. The output will thus be the input function negated.) Also F_2 is simply C, and its *or* gate can be replaced with a hard wire to C.

Since minterms 1 and 2 are never used, the two *and* gates corresponding to them can also be eliminated immediately.

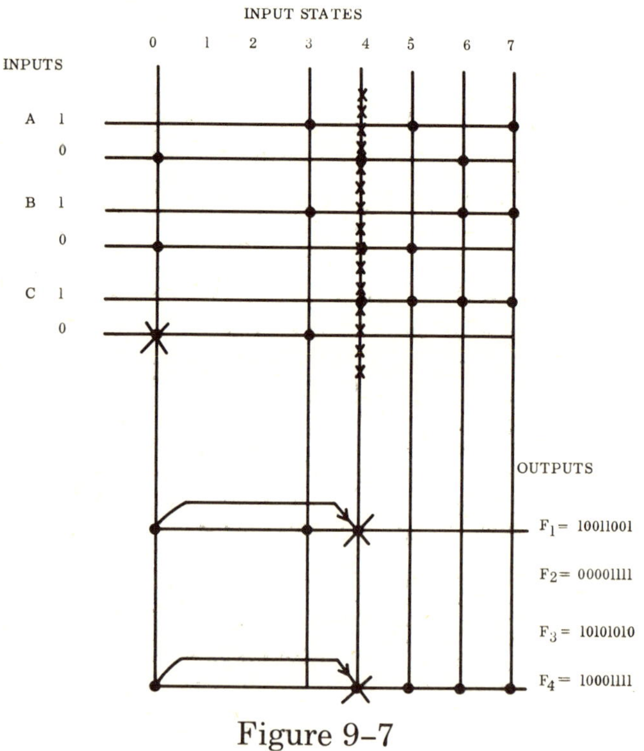

Figure 9–7

Figure 9–7 shows a method for further simplification. This method depends on looking for what are called implications. A is said to imply B if when A is true B is. This is denoted by $A \rightarrow B$. Note if A implies B, B does not have to imply A. If it in fact does, then $A = B$.

It can be seen from Figure 9–7 that state 0 implies state 4. In other words, for every dot in state 0 there is a dot on the same *or* gate in state 4. Therefore, the set of dots in state 0 is a subset of the set of dots in state 4. What is done mechanically is to draw an arrow from each dot in state 0 to the corresponding dot in state 4 and remove this dot in state 4. Having done this, m_4 is left out of F_1 and F_2. Obviously what is left is not the function specified. Therefore compensation must be made for this change. Looking at the minterms at the top of the matrix it is found that the input states for m_0 and m_4 have identical elements except that m_0 has a $\overline{C}$ term and m_4 has a C term. What is then done to compensate for the manipulations already made is to cross out the $\overline{C}$ dot for minterm 0.

This can be done mechanically, but the theory behind this manipulation can be seen by writing out the elementary products as follows:

$$m_0 = \overline{A} \cdot \overline{B} \cdot \overline{C} \qquad m_4 = \overline{A} \cdot \overline{B} \cdot C$$

Since state 0 (minterm 0) implies state 4 (minterm 4), it follows that these two terms are present together (on functions F_1 and F_4). Hence, they may be logically added:

$$\overline{A} \cdot \overline{B} \cdot \overline{C} + \overline{A} \cdot \overline{B} \cdot C$$

By factoring,

$$\overline{A} \cdot \overline{B}(\overline{C} + C)$$

But $(\overline{C} + C) = 1$

Therefore the expression reduces to:

$$\overline{A} \cdot \overline{B}$$

Thus, by removing the $\overline{C}$ dot from state 0 we have put $\overline{A} \cdot \overline{B}$ on functions 1 and 4 which is the equivalent of $m_0 + m_4$ which has been removed.

The general technique in simplifying the logic on a matrix is to keep looking for implications and treating them in the foregoing manner until no further implications can be found.

If enough implications can be found to eliminate all of the dots associated with a gate, the entire gate can be eliminated. In Figure 9–7 the *and* gate for m_4 has been eliminated. This method of dot elimination will produce the simplest logic possible. Figure 9–8 shows the final simplified logic.

Basic Circuits

Perhaps the easiest method of simplifying logic is the use of basic logic circuit building blocks of higher levels of complexity. There are certain basic logical devices that occur very frequently in logic

A
B
C
$\overline{A}\,\overline{B}$
$AB\overline{C}$
$F_1 = \overline{A}\,\overline{B} + AB\overline{C}$
= 10011001
$F_2 = C$
= 00001111
$F_3 = \overline{A}$
= 10101010
$A\overline{B}C$
$\overline{A}BC$
$F_4 = \overline{A}\,\overline{B} + A\overline{B}C +$
$\overline{A}BC + ABC$
= 10001111
ABC

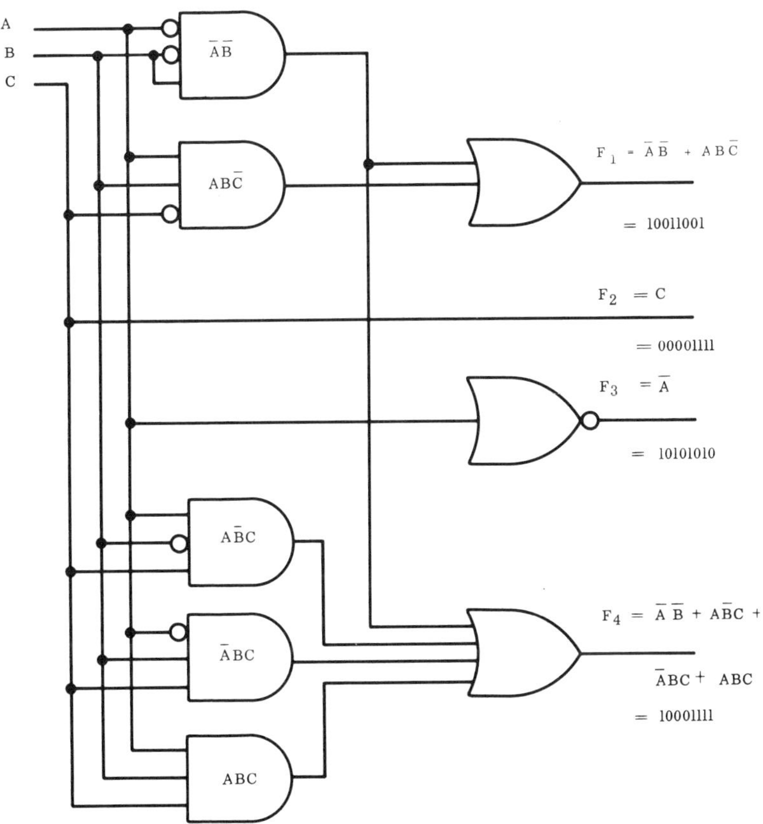

Figure 9–8

design, such as decimal counters, shift registers, etc. It is not necessary to redesign a counter every time an application requires one. Once a logic function is designed, it need never be redesigned, and more complex configurations may be put together by combining functions of considerably more complexity than basic *and* or *or* gates.

Not only can these basic combinations be utilized in logic design, but they can also be purchased as complete integrated circuits without actually having to build them up out of basic gates. Manufacturer's catalogues provide a very useful library of logic circuits available for specific functions and should always be consulted prior to the design of complex systems. A good designer does not design a system that has already been designed by someone else.

Being familiar with certain basic functions and how they may be implemented also includes being familiar with basic designation numbers. It can take a lot of gates to implement the function 00001111 if the designer does not recognize that it is simply input variable C in a three input system.

Chapter 10
A Practical Example

If the reader has followed all of the material presented in the previous chapters, he is probably wondering what all of the abstract concepts presented have to do with practical problems. It is certain that he does not realize the enormous design power that resides in the relatively simple logic design principles presented thus far. Thus, before going on, it may be desirable to illustrate how these principles can be utilized in a cookbook fashion to solve practical problems.

There are seven basic steps in logic design:

1. Define the problem. This can best be done by drawing a black box showing all of the required inputs and outputs and the relationship between them in a general way.
2. Write the standard basis for all input states.
3. Complete the truth table by filling in 1's and 0's in the designation numbers for all outputs in accordance with the requirements for the particular system.

4. Write out a logic expression for each output variable either directly from the designation number in terms of minterms or maxterms, or from a matrix if the system is complicated.
5. Use the methods of Chapter 9 to simplify the logic as much as possible.
6. Draw the resultant logic diagram.
7. Implement the system by assembling the hardware, and test and debug the system.

If it is intended to use nor or nand gates, then the additional step of converting the logic as written directly in terms of *and* and *or* gates to nor or nand logic will have to be undertaken at this point. This is most conveniently done directly from the logic diagram by adding double negations, as illustrated in Chapter 9.

As a concrete illustration of these basic steps, the detailed design of a system that is capable of computing the simple function $Y = 2X$ will be worked out (i.e., the output of the logic system must always be representative of a number twice that of the input).

Step 1

Since logic systems are binary devices, it follows that the input and output numbers must be binary numbers. Since the designer would not be likely to want to limit the input number, or X, to only 0 and 1, it follows that more than one bit is required to represent the input. For this problem assume that the input number can have any decimal value from 0 to 7. The highest possible value, 7, requires three binary digits or bits (i.e., 111). One very simple way of handling this problem is by the previously mentioned technique of assigning different weights to input variables. Input A can represent the least significant or 1 bit, input B can represent the 2 bit, and input C can represent the 4 bit. If the possible input, X, can vary between a value of 0 to 7, then a three input variable system is required.

Looking next at the required output, Y, its highest value must be $2 \times 7 = 14$. Using the same technique of assigning different weights to output variables, it is apparent that the number 14 requires four bits or output functions to represent it (i.e., 1110). Therefore, let F_1 represent the 1 bit, F_2 the 2 bit, F_3 the 4 bit, and F_4 the 8 bit. Figure 10–1 represents the resulting block diagram or black box configuration.

Step 2

State		0	1	2	3	4	5	6	7
A	(1)	0	1	0	1	0	1	0	1
B	(2)	0	0	1	1	0	0	1	1
C	(4)	0	0	0	0	1	1	1	1

The reader may have wondered in the past why state numbers start with 0 instead of 1. Now that all three input variables are taken to represent one binary number and have the weights as shown, the reason should be apparent. The vertical sequence of 1's and 0's in each column, when weighted as shown, add up to the binary equivalent of the state number. Thus in a four input system there would be 16 different state combinations $(0-15)$, and if input D were weighted as 8 the columns would still form the appropriate binary state numbers.

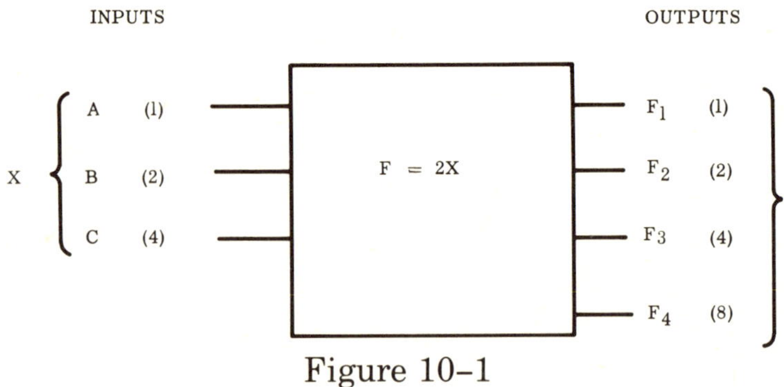

Figure 10–1

Step 3

This step involves the filling in of a 1 or a 0 for each bit of the designation numbers for each of the output functions. This is done in accordance with the design requirements by simply considering the weighted value of each output and putting 1's in each column such that the resulting output binary number is equal to twice the binary number represented by the inputs in the same column, as follows:

			0	1	2	3	4	5	6	7
	States		0	1	2	3	4	5	6	7
	A	(1)	0	1	0	1	0	1	0	1
Inputs	B	(2)	0	0	1	1	0	0	1	1
	C	(4)	0	0	0	0	1	1	1	1
	F_1	(1)	0	0	0	0	0	0	0	0
Outputs	F_2	(2)	0	1	0	1	0	1	0	1
	F_3	(4)	0	0	1	1	0	0	1	1
	F_4	(8)	0	0	0	0	1	1	1	1

For example, in state 5: 5 (101) × 2 = 10 (1010).

Steps 4 and 5

Steps 4 and 5 are combined because a look at the designation numbers in the above truth table is enough to simplify the logic by inspection. In the first place, it can be seen that the output 1 bit, F_1, is never used, and hence this output can be discarded. This should surprise no one since when multiplying by 2 the product must be an even number.

A further look at the designation numbers will disclose that F_2 is simply A, F_3 is B and F_4 is C. Hence all logic gates can be eliminated and replaced by three hard wires to the inputs. In effect all that need be done is to assign different weights to these three lines on the output end to achieve the $2X$ function.

This is obviously a special case. In order to illustrate these procedures in a more typical situation a system to multiply a three bit binary input number by 3 will now be designed. The maximum value of the output will be $3 \times 7 = 21$ (10101), and this will require five output functions, as shown in Figure 10-2.

Steps 2 and 3

$$Y = 3X$$

State		0	1	2	3	4	5	6	7
A	(1)	0	1	0	1	0	1	0	1
B	(2)	0	0	1	1	0	0	1	1
C	(4)	0	0	0	0	1	1	1	1
F_1	(1)	0	1	0	1	0	1	0	1
F_2	(2)	0	1	1	0	0	1	1	0
F_3	(4)	0	0	1	0	1	1	0	1
F_4	(8)	0	0	0	1	1	1	0	0
F_5	(16)	0	0	0	0	0	0	1	1
Decimal Equivalent of Output	0	3	6	9	12	15	18	21

The foregoing truth table was obtained exactly as it was in the $Y = 2X$ example except that here all columns in the output portion of the truth table represent binary numbers of three times the value of the input number above it. For example, in state 5: 5 (101) $\times$ 3 = 15 (01111).

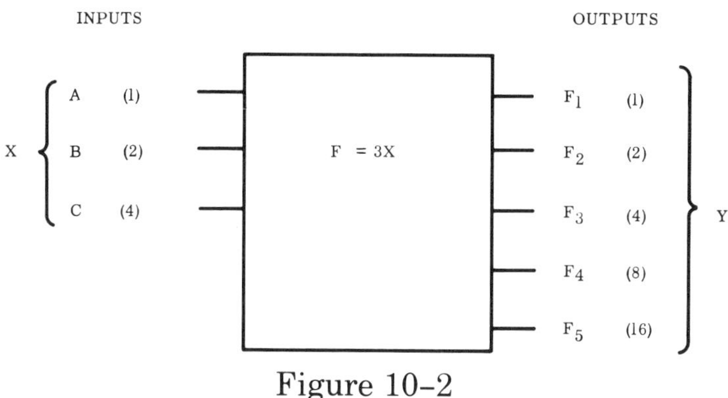

Figure 10–2

Step 4

Now proceed to write a separate logic statement for each output function. Since there are more 0's than 1's in the designation numbers, the use of minterms would produce the simpler initial logic. All that is needed is to write the appropriate minterms for each 1 in a designation number, one function at a time. If the reader has forgotten which minterm is which or the weighting system described as a mnemonic device, he now knows how to write minterms directly from a matrix as shown in Chapter 9.

Starting with F_1 it is discovered that it is not necessary to use minterms for this function as it has the same designation number as input A. Hence, $F_1 = A$.

$$F_2 = m_1 + m_2 + m_5 + m_6$$
$$F_3 = m_2 + m_4 + m_5 + m_7$$
$$F_4 = m_3 + m_4 + m_5$$
$$F_5 = m_6 + m_7$$

The reason that these functions were written first in minterm notation is that this practice makes it easier to recognize common gates between functions; for example, m_2 is used twice as is m_4, and m_5 appears three times. Naturally only one gate is required for these multiple functions.

The full logic statements may be written in *and*-to-*or* logic as follows:

$$F_1 = A$$

$$
\begin{aligned}
F_2 &= A\cdot\overline{B}\cdot\overline{C} &+& \quad \overline{A}\cdot B\cdot\overline{C} &+& \quad A\cdot\overline{B}\cdot C &+& \quad \overline{A}\cdot B\cdot C \\
&= m_1 &+& \quad m_2 &+& \quad m_5 &+& \quad m_6 \\
F_3 &= \overline{A}\cdot B\cdot\overline{C} &+& \quad \overline{A}\cdot\overline{B}\cdot C &+& \quad A\cdot\overline{B}\cdot C &+& \quad A\cdot B\cdot C \\
&= m_2 &+& \quad m_4 &+& \quad m_5 &+& \quad m_7 \\
F_4 &= A\cdot B\cdot\overline{C} &+& \quad \overline{A}\cdot\overline{B}\cdot C &+& \quad A\cdot\overline{B}\cdot C \\
&= m_3 &+& \quad m_4 &+& \quad m_5 \\
F_5 &= \overline{A}\cdot B\cdot C &+& \quad A\cdot B\cdot C \\
&= m_6 &+& \quad m_7
\end{aligned}
$$

Step 5

Using Boolean algebra to simplify the logic, we look for terms that can be factored to yield an expression of the form $(A + \overline{A}) \cdot (X)$ which will then simplify to just (X). For example, in F_2 minterms 1 and 5 can have the common element $A \cdot \overline{B}$ factored out yielding: $(A \cdot \overline{B})(C + \overline{C}) = A \cdot \overline{B}$. Also minterms 2 and 6 can have the common term $\overline{A} \cdot B$ factored out yielding $(\overline{A} \cdot B)(C + \overline{C}) = \overline{A} \cdot B$. Therefore F_2 reduces to:

$$F_2 = A \cdot \overline{B} \; + \; \overline{A} \cdot B$$

If the reader thinks about it, he will realize that this elimination of a variable by combining minterm gates is exactly what was done in a more mechanical way when dots were eliminated on a matrix by looking for implications.

By the same technique, m_4 and m_5 of F_3 can be combined by taking out the common factor $\overline{B} \cdot C$ and writing $(\overline{B} \cdot C) (A + \overline{A}) = \overline{B} \cdot C$. Therefore,

$$F_3 = \overline{A} \cdot B \cdot \overline{C} \; + \; \overline{B} \cdot C \; + \; A \cdot B \cdot C$$

Since F_4 contains the same m_4 and m_5 gates as F_3 (which have already been shown to combine to yield $\overline{B} \cdot C$), we can write F_4 in simplified form:

$$F_4 = A \cdot B \cdot \overline{C} \; + \; \overline{B} \cdot C$$

By the same technique, F_5 can be factored into:

$$(B \cdot C)(A + \overline{A}) = BC$$

Step 6

Now that the *and*-to-*or* logic is in its simplest form, a logic diagram of the system can be written directly as shown in Figure 10–3.

The logic diagram of Figure 10–3 may be directly implemented using *and* and *or* gates as sup-

A
B
C
$F_1 = A$
$F_2 = A \cdot \bar{B} + \bar{A} \cdot B$
$F_3 = \bar{A}\,B\,\bar{C} + \bar{B}\,C + A\,B\,C$
$F_4 = A\,B\,\bar{C} + \bar{B}\,C$
$F_5 = B\,C$
$A\bar{B}$
$\bar{A}B$
$\bar{A}B\bar{C}$
$\bar{B}C$
ABC
$AB\bar{C}$
BC

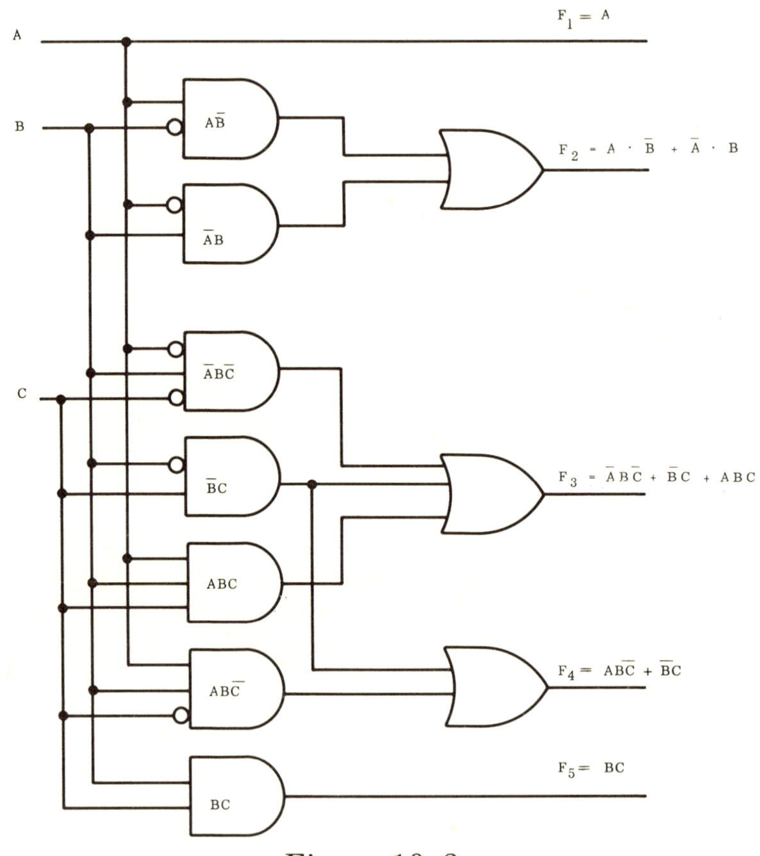

Figure 10–3

A
B
C
$F_1 = A$
$\overline{A\overline{B}}$
$\overline{\overline{A}B}$
$F_2 = A \cdot \overline{B} + \overline{A} \cdot B$
$\overline{\overline{A}B\overline{C}}$
$\overline{\overline{B}C}$
$\overline{AB\overline{C}}$
$F_3 = \overline{A}B\overline{C} + \overline{B}C + ABC$
$\overline{A\overline{B}\overline{C}}$
$F_4 = AB\overline{C} + \overline{B}C$
$\overline{BC}$
$F_5 = BC$

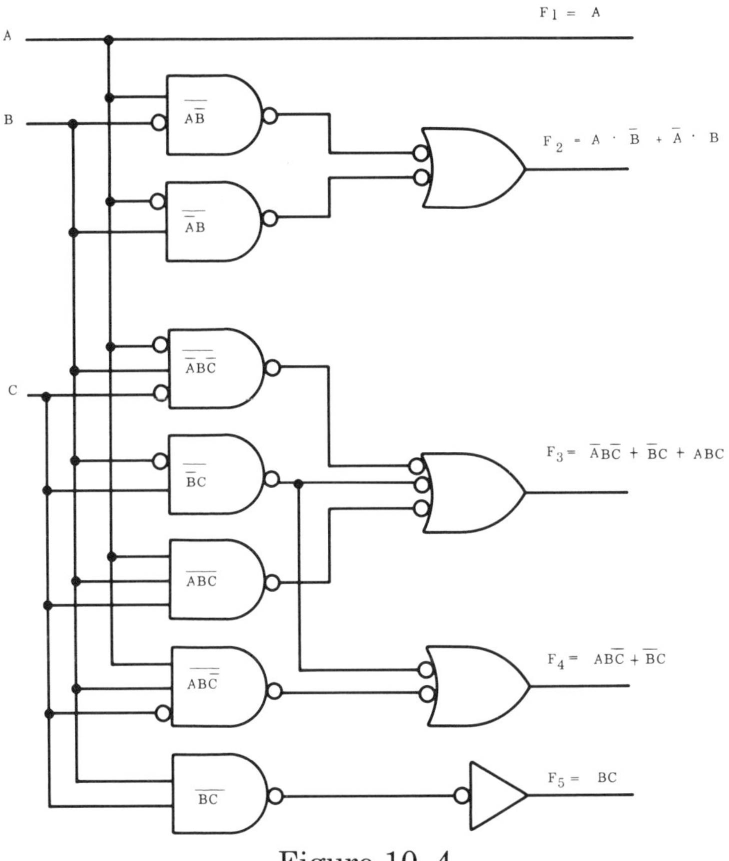

Figure 10–4

F1 = A
F2 = (A · B̄) (Ā · B)
= A·B̄ + Ā·B
AB̄
ĀB
ABC̄
B̄C
ABC
F3 = (ABC̄) (B̄C) (ABC)
= ABC̄ + B̄C + ABC
ABC̄
F4 = (B̄C) (ABC̄)
= B̄C + ABC̄
BC
F5 = BC
= BC
A
B
C

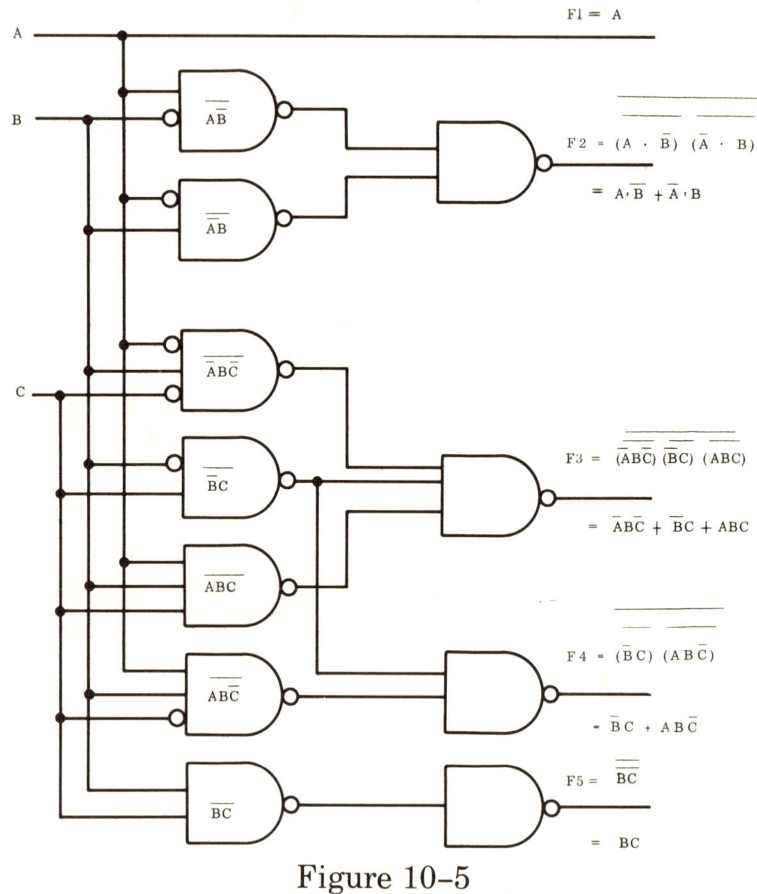

Figure 10–5

plied by manufacturers of laboratory equipment for behavioral laboratories, but if it is desired to use the much cheaper commercially available μ-logic packages the system of Figure 10–3 should be converted into nand logic by double negation of the *and* gate outputs, as shown in Figure 10–4, to get the nand gate system of Figure 10–5. Since commercial gates do not come supplied with input negation, an inverter will be needed for each input variable requiring negation. However, only one inverter is needed no matter how many times the inverted variable is used.

As an exercise the reader should try to do steps 2 through 5 of this design by the matrix method. This will give a better feeling for the advantages and disadvantages of both methods of design and will give some insight into the equivalence of the different techniques available. Which technique is preferable depends on the individual problem and somewhat on personal taste, but in a complicated system such as this one the matrix method will prove more direct and easier to most people.

If it were now desired to design a more complicated computing device, such as one to solve the equation $Y = 2X + 3$, for values of X ranging from 0 to 7, there are two possible approaches available. One way is to design the system *ab initio* with each of the output states representing a binary number of the value $2X + 3$ in the truth table. Another method is to use the device already designed and feed its output into another black box that simply adds 3 to its value. Which method is simpler can be determined by working out the design both ways. However, in a case where the same basic function is repeated often, the latter method may be a work saver. The most important personality characteristic of a good designer is that he must be lazy.

Chapter 11
Pulses

Up to this point gates and their functioning have been discussed without regard to the dimension of time. It was more or less tacitly assumed that an input was either in the 1 or 0 state and that it stayed in that state indefinitely. If a 1 represents the closure of a micro switch connected to the bar of a Skinner box and a 0 represents the switch being open, it is obvious that this input can have different states at different periods of time. In this case it is also apparent that the time duration of the 1 and 0 state can be quite erratic, with the 0's tending to be of variable duration but in general quite long while the 1's will tend to be momentary or transient states.

In logic systems in general, as will become apparent in the next chapter, events tend to occur sequentially, and the system performs different functions at different times. The coordination of these activities is usually accomplished by means of what is called a clock pulse. In order to better appreciate what a clock or timing pulse is, consider the four graphs shown in Figure 11–1. For all four figures, the abscissa represents time and the ordinate represents voltage.

Graph A in Figure 11–1 shows a positive going pulse. As can be seen, the voltage jumps from 0 to some positive value at time $= 0$, remains there for a period of time, and then returns to 0. In positive logic, the higher voltage-on period would correspond to a logical 1, and the voltage-off period would correspond to a logical 0. With negative logic, the situation would be just the reverse.

Graph B shows a negative going pulse of equal time duration. In this case the 0 voltage level would correspond to a logical 1, and the pulse on period would correspond to a logical 0 in positive logic. In both cases, the pulse is said to be on when the graph leaves the baseline and off when it returns to it. Note that these graphs show only two levels: pulse on or off. This is because the system is a binary system, and these are by definition the only two states possible.

Graphs C and D show the beginnings of a positive and negative going pulse respectively, but in these cases the "pulse" does not return to the base line. Hence, these are not pulses at all but represent permanent on or off signals such as have been discussed prior to this chapter. After a period of time, these signals may eventually be returned to the base line (for example, when a subject closed a switch), but since they do not have a definite time duration they are not classified as pulses.

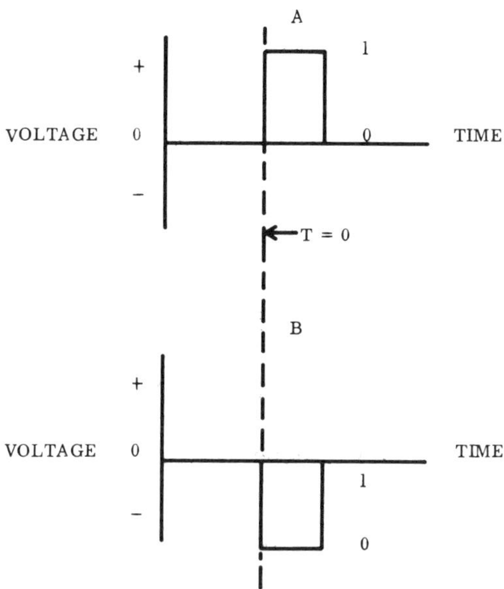

Figure 11-1, parts A & B

A study of Graph A discloses the major characteristics of all pulses. The first characteristic is its amplitude. This will depend on the voltage levels chosen to represent logical 1's and 0's in the system. Values of ±5 or ±12 volts are typical. The base line of the pulse represents the logical 0 level, and this does not have to be at 0 volts.

The second major characteristic of a pulse is its duration, or pulse width as it is called. This is specified in some unit of time such as a millisecond (10^{-3} seconds) a μ second (10^{-6} seconds), or a nanosecond (10^{-9} seconds).

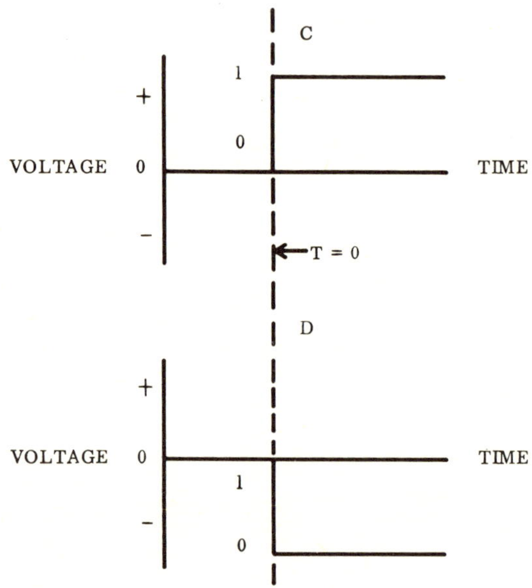

Figure 11–1, parts C & D

Graph A shows an ideal pulse that is impossible to attain in practice. The graph shows the pulse starting at $t = 0$ and attaining its full value instantly. It also shows the pulse going to 0 instantly at its conclusion. Due to the presence of lead inductance in any electrical circuit a certain amount of time is required for a pulse to build up or decay, and the shorter the pulse duration the more significant this rise time and fall time, as it's called, becomes. Since a pulse does not come on instantly, some standard is needed to define when it is on or off. Considering the leading edge of the pulse (i.e., the portion on the left of the diagram which occurs first in time), the rise time is taken as that period of time necessary for the pulse to attain 90% of its steady value. On the trailing edge of the pulse, the fall time is taken as the time required for the pulse to decay to 10% of its full value. The manufacturers of gates and flip flop devices that operate from pulsed signals will specify at what voltage levels these devices will switch, or toggle as its called. Thus while a logical 1 in a particular system may be nominally specified as +12 volts dc, there is a specific range given over which the device will still work properly in spite of minor fluctuations of voltage.

Pulse width is actually measured between the two lowest levels of voltage that will represent the logical 1 level at the leading and trailing edges of the pulse.

While not apparent from Figure 11–1, pulses may occur randomly or regularly in a system. For example, in the Skinner box example the period that the micro switch is depressed may be too erratic to work the equipment properly. Hence, we may put this switch closure through a device, like a one shot multivibrator, which will take this variable closure time and give a single pulse output having just the pulse characteristics wanted for the system. The timing of the occurrence of these nicely shaped pulses, however, will be completely erratic depending on the rat's behavior.

Sometimes pulses may be generated regularly to provide timing for system operations. In such a case they are called clock pulses, and the number of these pulses per second is called the repetition, or rep, rate.

In general the period that a pulse is on will be unequal to the period that it is off (but not always). The ratio of time-on to time-off is referred to as the duty cycle of the pulse.

The most common ways of generating a clock pulse is to use either a device called a free running multivibrator which generates a recurrent pulse or an ordinary oscillator circuit which generates a recurrent frequency. The output of an oscillator can then be shaped into any kind of pulse needed by the use of the devices described in Chapter 12.

While modern computer systems can function at extremely high speeds, and thus use very short pulse times, such systems require the use of special techniques, and the experimental apparatus designer is not likely ever to get involved with such problems.

Even at fairly low clock frequencies, however, the designer must be aware of the problem of stray capacity and inductance in a circuit, for Fourier's theorem states that any nonsinusoidal recurrent wave shape can be resolved into a series of harmonically related pure sine waves starting at the fundamental frequency and continuing upward. Thus, a square wave or pulse represents many higher frequency harmonics even if the rep rate is quite low. This is the reason why pulse shape deteriorates when passing through several passive gates, and why active ones, like nor or nand gates, are preferable to *or* or *and* gates in actual circuits. These active devices not only function as gates but they regenerate or reshape the pulse as it travels through them and eliminate concern with this problem.

Chapter 12
Signal Conditioning and Input Interfacing

Now that the characteristics of clock and other pulses have been described, it is necessary to show where these pulses originate in the typical logic system. There are two basic sources for pulses:

1. A switch closure associated with some manipulanda.
2. A clock oscillator or multivibrator.

Let us consider the former case first. As will be shown later, many logical devices such as flip flops and counters function better when driven with pulses as opposed to steady state signal levels. Since in general the inputs to a logic system used in a piece of psychological experimental apparatus will result from the operation of some manipulanda by a subject or an experimental animal, it is desirable to convert this input into a pulse form. The manipulanda themselves will usually be mechanically ganged to a switch which will provide a switch closure or a steady state output level when operated.

INPUT
OUTPUT
INTEGRATOR
DIFFERENTIATOR
ST
SCHMITT TRIGGER
OS
ONE SHOT MV

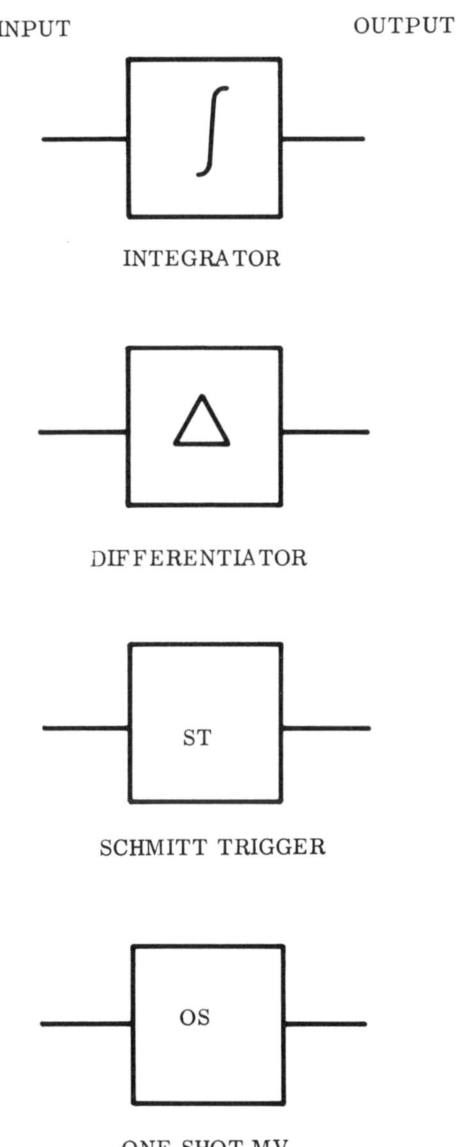

Figure 12–1

To convert this steady state signal level (which may be quite long or short in duration) to a standard shaped pulse involves the use of several nonbinary components that might be called signal conditioning devices. Four basic devices will be discussed in this chapter, and Figure 12–1 shows the conventional logic diagram symbols used to denote them. There will be no concern here with the electronic circuitry involved in performing these functions, but they will be considered from an input–output or functional standpoint, i.e., what transformation is made on an input signal to produce the output signal. These four devices are called: a Schmitt trigger, a monostable multivibrator or a single shot multivibrator, an integrator, and a differentiator.

A Schmitt trigger is a pulse shaping device. It functions basically as a voltage level detector. Thus, whenever the input voltage is above the level that the trigger is set for, it puts out an assertion or 1 level signal for as long as the voltage is above the triggering threshold. When the voltage falls below this threshold, the Schmitt trigger will put out a negation or 0 level signal. Thus, it is capable of taking a sine wave (or any complex wave) input signal and converting it into a square shaped pulse output. The output or 1 level of the Schmitt trigger must be set to be compatible with the 1 level of the logic gates used. Hence, a Schmitt trigger is ideally suited to square up a pulse whose edges have become deteriorated or curved as a result of passing through several passive gates. In logic involving nor or nand gates where active elements are used, the pulse is reshaped at each gate, and hence Schmitt triggers are not needed for pulse reshaping. But note carefully that the pulse width of the output of a Schmitt trigger is determined solely by how long the input voltage is above the triggering threshold, and hence the pulse width is not constant.

A one shot multivibrator is used to generate a pulse with a standard pulse width. This is a device which when driven with an input above its threshold of operation will produce one pulse of standard duration regardless of how long the input is held on. After the input is removed, if it is reapplied a second standard pulse will be produced.

Thus, a Schmitt trigger would be used to generate a pulse if the pulse width was required to vary with the input signal on-time (i.e., if the input signal on-time was correct for the application). A one shot would be used to generate a pulse having a precise time duration regardless of the time of input signal duration.

Therefore, to generate a standardized pulse for a logic control system from the pressing of a bar in a Skinner box a one shot multivibrator is used. The bar is used to close a switch which puts an input of uncertain duration on a one shot. The one shot then yields one standardized pulse output for each bar press.

Integrators and differentiators are circuits which perform the mathematical functions of integration and differentiation, respectively.

More specifically, an integrator is a circuit whose output level is a function of how long an input signal is applied as well as how strong it is. Hence, this is an ideal device to be used as a filter to eliminate outputs due to transient signals while deriving outputs from longer or steady state signals. Thus, an integrator can be used to require that a signal have some minimum time duration before a system will respond to it. Since the integrator provides a varing output voltage level as opposed to a binary type 1 or 0 level, it is necessary to feed the output of an integrator to a Schmitt trigger or one shot to get a binary level signal. If a steady state signal in binary form is wanted, a Schmitt trigger would be used. If a standard time based pulse is wanted, a one shot would be used.

A differentiator is a device giving an output voltage level that is a function of the rate of change of the input signal level. Since it also produces a nonbinary output, it must also be used in conjunction with a Schmitt trigger or one shot if it is to be used in a binary system.

It should be realized that the inputs and outputs of binary systems in general are voltage levels quite different from those representing binary 1's or 0's. Hence, some types of interfacing devices are needed to connect up the total system. For outputs the most common interfacing devices used are relays or operational amplifiers, while Schmitt triggers and one shots are the common interfacing devices on the input side.

With respect to the second source of pulses, i.e., clock pulses, these are often generated by a device called an oscillator. If a precise time base or reference is needed, a crystal controlled oscillator will be used which yields a highly accurate frequency output. If such accuracy is not required, a variable oscillator may be used to give an adjustable time base. Since the output of an oscillator is a sine wave, this output must be fed through a squaring device like a Schmitt trigger to give a pulsed output of alternating 1 and 0 levels. Note that in this case a Schmitt trigger is preferable to a one shot for here the time base accuracy is being supplied by the oscillator.

Chapter 13
Recursive Systems

A recursive system is one that sequentially changes outputs and in which the inputs at time N are a function of the outputs at time $N-1$. In other words, it is a system involving time delayed feedback. Since sequential output states are being considered for the first time, it is necessary to realize that it takes a finite time for an input, whether pulsed or steady state, to pass through a gate. In a modern integrated circuit package this time is quite small, on the order of less than 30 nanoseconds, but the actual values vary for different commercially available packages and must always be taken into account. This transit time (δ) or unit delay is for a single gate, and the total delay time is, of course, the gate transit time multiplied by the number of stages in the system.

To illustrate a recursive circuit, let us design a very useful device called a decimal counter. This is a system that sequentially counts in binary numbers from 0 to 10 and then repeats this cycle continu-

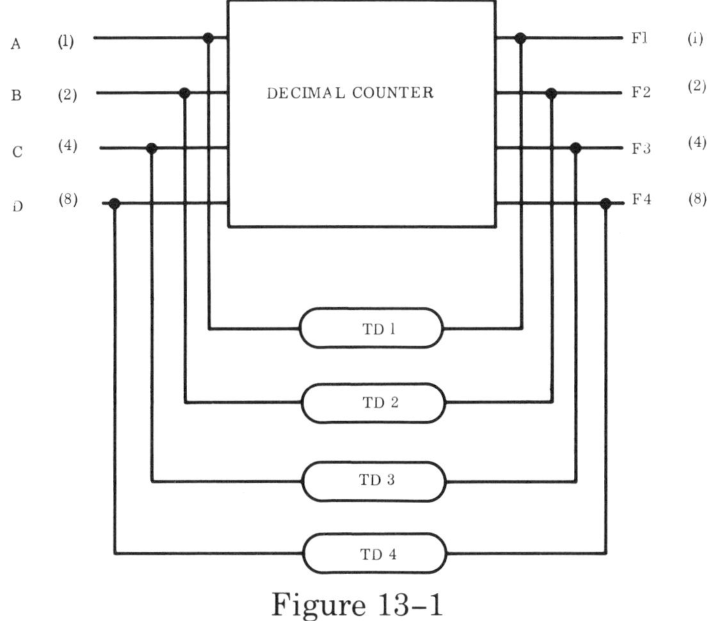

Figure 13-1

ously. Such a device has the potential of being used as the basic element in a clock or a timer which can be the basis for all kinds of temporally controlled equipment. For example decimal counters could be used to generate fixed interval schedules in a Skinner box.

The modulus of a counter is the number it counts to before repeating the sequence, and thus a decimal counter is a modulus 10 counter. Figure 13-1 shows the block diagram for a decimal counter.

Since it is desired to count to 10 in binary numbers and since each output is to represent a bit in a binary number, it follows that four output functions are needed. (The highest possible binary number expressible with three bits is 7, while with four bits it is 15). Since four bits are to be used, and the counter is to count to 10, not 15, logic must be used to somehow cut the count short at 10 and recycle the counter.

It is apparent from Figure 13–1 that each output line (which represents a binary bit) is fed back to the input line, representing the same bit, through a device whose sole function is to produce a time delay (TD). Thus, each output state will be the next input state. To produce such a counter all that need be done is to specify the logic in such a manner that if the input states represent the number N, then the output states will be $N + 1$. This requirement can be written directly into each column of the truth table as shown in Table 13–1.

Table 13–1

State	0	1	2	3	4	5	6	7	8	9	10	11	12	13	14	15
A	0	1	0	1	0	1	0	1	0	1	0	1	0	1	0	1
B	0	0	1	1	0	0	1	1	0	0	1	1	0	0	1	1
C	0	0	0	0	1	1	1	1	0	0	0	0	1	1	1	1
D	0	0	0	0	0	0	0	0	1	1	1	1	1	1	1	1
F_1	1	0	1	0	1	0	1	0	1	0	0	x	x	x	x	x
F_2	0	1	1	0	0	1	1	0	0	1	0	x	x	x	x	x
F_3	0	0	0	1	1	1	1	0	0	0	0	x	x	x	x	x
F_4	0	0	0	0	0	0	0	1	1	1	0	x	x	x	x	x

Notice that in the output column of state 10, instead of writing the binary number for 11, the number for 0 has been written. This will recycle the counter and start it off counting from 0 through 10 again. A little thought will convince the reader that by using the same programing technique a counter can be made to count in any sequence desired, up, down, by twos or in any irregular sequence. If it were desired to have the same number appear twice in the sequence (e.g., 2, 8, 5, 9, 5, 4), an additional bit would be needed to distinguish the first 5 from the second. This bit would not be part of the weighted outputs representing the output number, but would merely be used to prevent the first 5 from generating an output of 4 or the second one from generating an output of 9.

It should also be noted that there are no external inputs in this system. Signals A, B, C, and D represent the output functions fed back through time delays. These time delays must, as a minimum, delay the signal for a period longer than the transit time of all of the logic gates. Time delays may be purchased separately, but basically they can be made up of several of the slowest, cheapest *or* gates available. The time delays will determine the presentation time of each output number displayed. One of the problems that may be encountered in a recursive counter may be inequality in the time delays. This can result in undesirable transient states, which is one of the reasons why most counters are made up with flip flops.

A look at the truth table for this system discloses that state 11 through 15 are never entered, and hence the portions of the designation numbers representing these states have been marked with an X. Obviously these states that we "don't care" about must be represented by either a 0 or 1 in the function designation number, but the choice is completely arbitrary. Such a condition is called a constraint. The term is a poor one for it implies that this restricts the design in some way. Actually it is a very desirable state of affairs for any state can be assigned to these bits. It is like a wild card in poker. Constraints are usually resolved so that the simplest possible logic results. For example, if minterm or *and*-to-*or* logic is used, a 0 eliminates a gate. The situation is just the reverse for maxterm or *or*-to-*and* logic. Sometimes even with minterm logic, adding a 1 will simplify the logic. For example the designation number 01010X reduces to *A* if the X is resolved with a 1.

It is a cardinal rule of logic design that all constraints must be resolved. The reason for this is that if as the result of some transient condition the counter did get into one of the constrained states and if it were not resolved properly the system could cease to operate. By resolving all of the constrained states in the decimal counter with 0's, this possibility has been taken care of. More specifically, if somehow the counter got into state 12, it will now go back to 0 and resume counting correctly. If on the other hand this constrained state had been resolved with all 1's, the next count would be 15, and the following one would depend on how the constraints in state 15 were resolved. If they in turn were resolved with the binary equivalent of state 6, the next cycle would start at state 6. Besides simplifying the logic, constraints have to be considered with an eye to preventing possible system malfunctions from being aggravated.

The designation numbers for the output functions lead to the following minterm expressions for each function:

$$F_1 = \quad \overline{m_0 \qquad\qquad + \quad m_2}$$
$$+ \quad \overline{m_4 \qquad\qquad + \quad m_6}$$
$$+ \quad m_8$$

$$= \quad A \cdot \overline{B} \cdot \overline{C} \cdot \overline{D} \; + \; \overline{A} \cdot B \cdot \overline{C} \cdot \overline{D}$$
$$+ \; \overline{A} \cdot \overline{B} \cdot C \cdot \overline{D} \; + \; \overline{A} \cdot B \cdot C \cdot \overline{D}$$
$$+ \; \overline{A} \cdot \overline{B} \cdot \overline{C} \cdot D$$

$$= \quad (B + \overline{B})\overline{A} \cdot \overline{C} \cdot \overline{D}$$
$$+ \; (B + \overline{B})\overline{A} \cdot C \cdot \overline{D}$$
$$+ \; \overline{A} \cdot \overline{B} \cdot \overline{C} \cdot D$$

$$= \quad \overline{A} \cdot \overline{C} \cdot \overline{D} \; + \; \overline{A} \cdot C \cdot \overline{D}$$
$$+ \; \overline{A} \cdot \overline{B} \cdot \overline{C} \cdot D$$

F = DECIMAL COUNTER
D
C
A
B
ACD
ACD
ABCD
TD-1
F1 (1)
ABC
ABCD
ABCD
ABCD
TD-2
F2 (2)
ABCD
BCD
TD-3
F3 (4)
ABCD
BCD
TD-4
F4 (8)
4 OR GATES
11 AND GATES
4 TD'S (= 2D)
2 STAGES

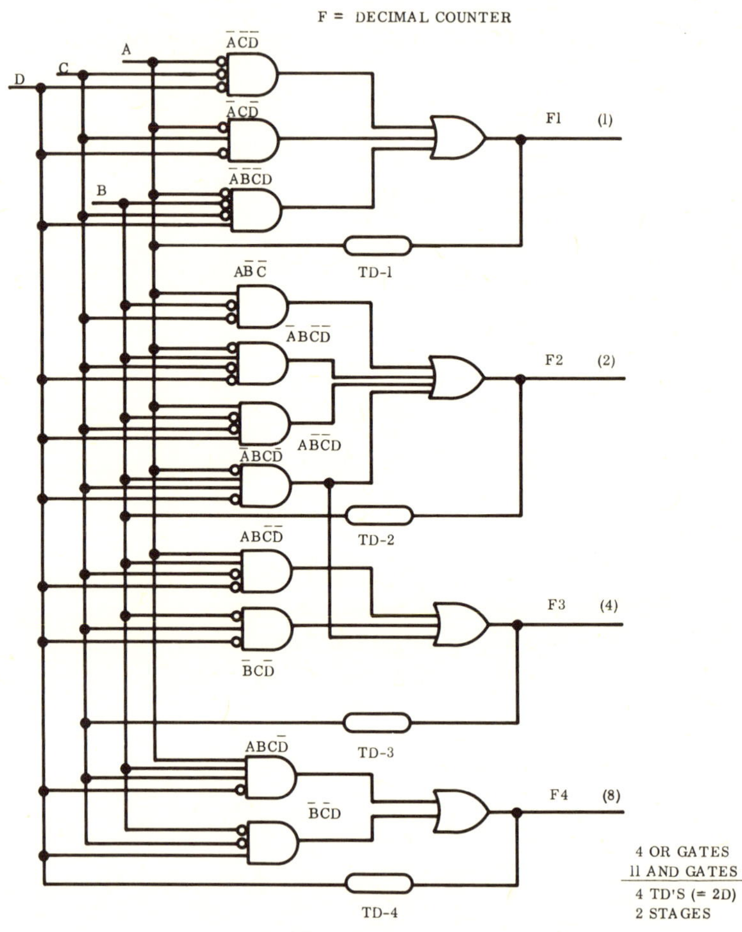

Figure 13-2

By the same type of factoring, the bracketed minterms also "factor," and the logic expressions reduce to the final statements shown under each statement in minterm form. As an exercise, the reader should write out each minterm and factor them to get the form shown.

$$F_2 = \overline{m_1 + m_2 + m_5 + m_6} + m_9$$
$$= A \cdot \overline{B} \cdot \overline{C} \; + \; \overline{A} \cdot B \cdot \overline{C} \cdot \overline{D} \; + \; A \cdot \overline{B} \cdot \overline{C} \cdot D$$
$$+ \; \overline{A} \cdot B \cdot C \cdot \overline{D}$$

$$F_3 = m_3 + \overline{m_4 + m_5} + m_6$$
$$= A \cdot B \cdot \overline{C} \cdot \overline{D} \; + \; \overline{B} \cdot C \cdot \overline{D} \; + \; \overline{A} \cdot B \cdot C \cdot \overline{D}$$

$$F_4 = m_7 + \overline{m_8 + m_9}$$
$$= A \cdot B \cdot C \cdot \overline{D} \; + \; \overline{B} \cdot \overline{C} \cdot D$$

Figure 13–2 represents the logic diagram for the decimal counter just designed in *and*-to-*or* form.

If the reader will study the "final" functions derived, he will notice that they can be further simplified by additional factoring; e.g.,

$$F_1 = (\overline{A} \cdot \overline{C} \cdot \overline{D}) \, (\overline{A} \cdot C \cdot \overline{D}) + (\overline{A} \cdot \overline{B} \cdot \overline{C} \; D)$$
$$= (\overline{A} \cdot \overline{D}) + (\overline{A} \cdot \overline{B} \cdot \overline{C} \cdot D)$$
$$= \overline{A}(\overline{D} + \overline{B} \cdot \overline{C} \cdot D)$$

It is left as an exercise for the reader to reduce the logic to its simplest form and to draw the final logic diagram.

Chapter 14
Flip Flops

Next to the basic gates (*and, or,* nand, and nor) and inverters, the most important and ubiquitous logical device is the flip flop or, as it is more formally called, the bistable multivibrator. This unit finds widespread application in all kinds of counters and shift registers and makes possible a wide variety of timing control circuitry.

THE RS OR SET-RESET FLIP FLOP

There are a variety of different types of flip flops, but the most basic is the RS or set-reset type. Figure 14–1 shows the block diagram of an RS flip flop.

The device has two inputs labeled R and S and two outputs labeled Q and $\overline{Q}$. Sometimes the Q output is labeled 1, and the $\overline{Q}$ is output is labeled 0.

The operation of a flip flop like any other logic system is defined by its truth table:

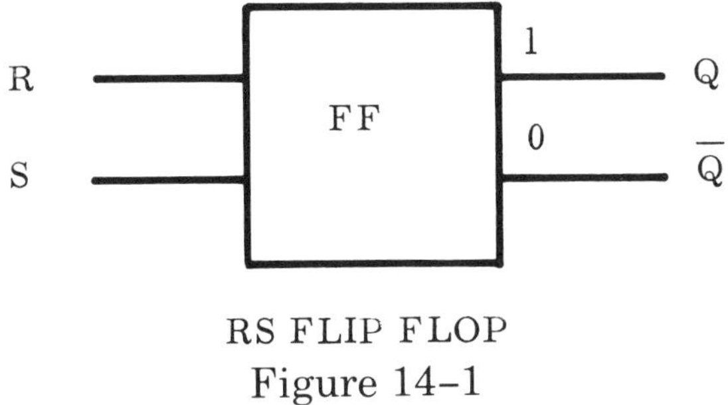

RS FLIP FLOP
Figure 14–1

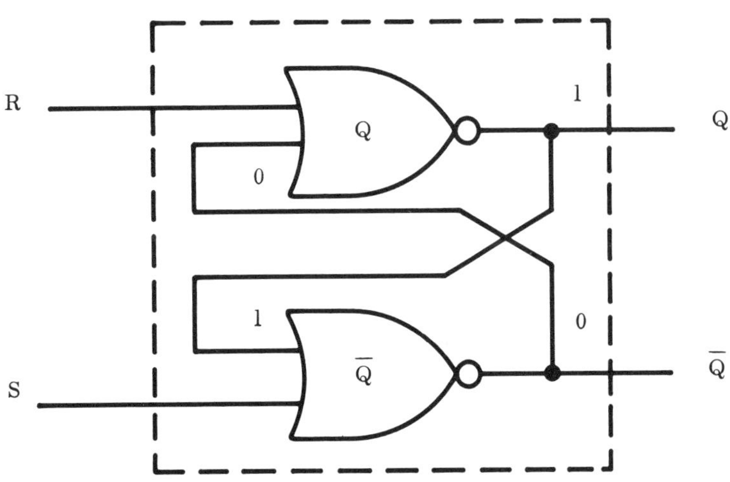

RS FLIP FLOP IN SET STATE
Figure 14–2

R		0	1	0	1
S		0	0	1	1
Q		Q_{N-1}	0	1	X
$\overline{Q}$		$\overline{Q}_{N-1}$	1	0	X

In the rest state where both R and S have 0's on them, the outputs will be in whatever state they were in last (i.e., it requires a 1 on either R or S to get a flip flop to change state or toggle).

Except for brief transitory periods while a flip flop is changing state, Q and $\overline{Q}$ are always the complement, or the opposite, of each other as the notation implies. When a reset signal R arrives, the flip flop is toggled into the output state where $Q = 0$ and $\overline{Q} = 1$. When a set, or S, signal arrives, the flip flop toggles into the second possible state where $Q = 1$ and $\overline{Q} = 0$.

When a flip flop's outputs are labeled 1 and 0, instead of Q and $\overline{Q}$, it does not mean that the 1 line always has a 1 on it. This is only true when the device is in the set state.

The X's in the truth table for the position where both R and S are in the 1 state indicate that this is a condition that must never occur and if by error it did occur the condition of the flip flop is not predictable.

While the flip flops are usually purchased as complete integrated circuits, they can be made from a pair of nor gates as shown in Figure 14–2. A study of this figure will cast light on the operation of a flip flop without regard to the particular circuitry involved in the individual gates. The flip flop is shown in the set condition with $Q=1$ and $\overline{Q}=0$. This puts a 0 on one input of nor gate Q and a 1 on one input of nor gate $\overline{Q}$. Lines R and S are in the resting condition with no input on either.

Since the flip flop is in the set condition, a set signal coming in on line S should have no effect on the state of the flip flop. A study of Figure 14–2 shows this to be the case, since a 1 on S would simply put two 1's on nor gate $\overline{Q}$ which would change nothing.

On the other hand if a reset pulse arrived, a 1 would be put on nor gate Q. This would result in the output of this gate changing from 1 to 0 after a time delay of δ. This in turn would replace the 1 input to nor gate $\overline{Q}$ with a 0, which will cause its output to change from 0 to 1 after an additional time delay of δ.

Thus an R signal applied to a flip flop in the set condition causes it to change to the opposite or reset state after a time delay of 2δ (2 times the transit time per gate). It should also be noted that after the first interval of δ both the Q and $\overline{Q}$ lines have the same level until the end of the second δ interval.

Figure 14–3 shows the flip flop of Figure 14–2 in the reset condition. Since the flip flop is reset, it follows that an incoming reset pulse should not change things. As can be seen from Figure 14–3, an incoming 1 on the R line will simply put a second 1 on nor gate Q which will change nothing.

An incoming S pulse, however, will flip the out-

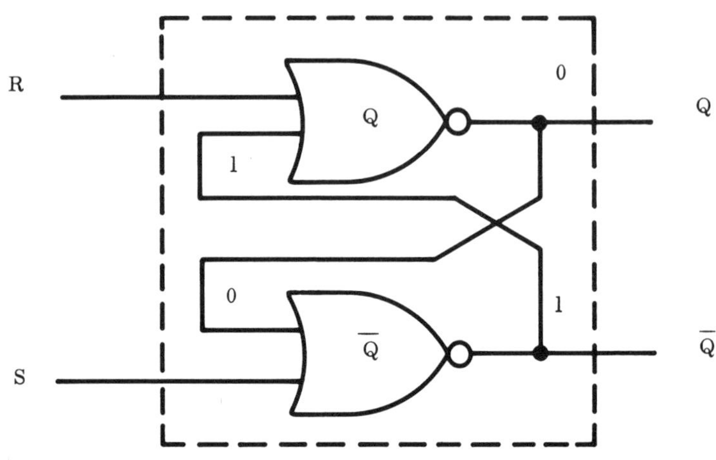

RS FLIP FLOP IN RESET STATE

Figure 14-3

put of nor gate $\overline{Q}$ from 1 to 0 after a time delay of δ. This will then change the input line on nor gate Q from 1 to 0 which will result in the output of this gate flopping from 0 to 1 after an additional delay of δ.

Figure 14-4 is a timing diagram showing the time sequence of the various changes of states when an initially reset flip flop is toggled into the set state by an incoming S pulse. As an exercise, the reader should prepare a similar diagram for an initially set flip flop being reset.

There are many other types of flip flops, some of which will be described briefly in this chapter. They

1
0
R
TIME
1
0
S
TIME
1
0
Q
TIME
1
0
Q̄
TIME
δ
δ
2 δ
T = 0
T = 0 + 2 δ
PULSE WIDTH ≥ 2 δ
TIMING DIAGRAM FOR RS FLIP FLOP

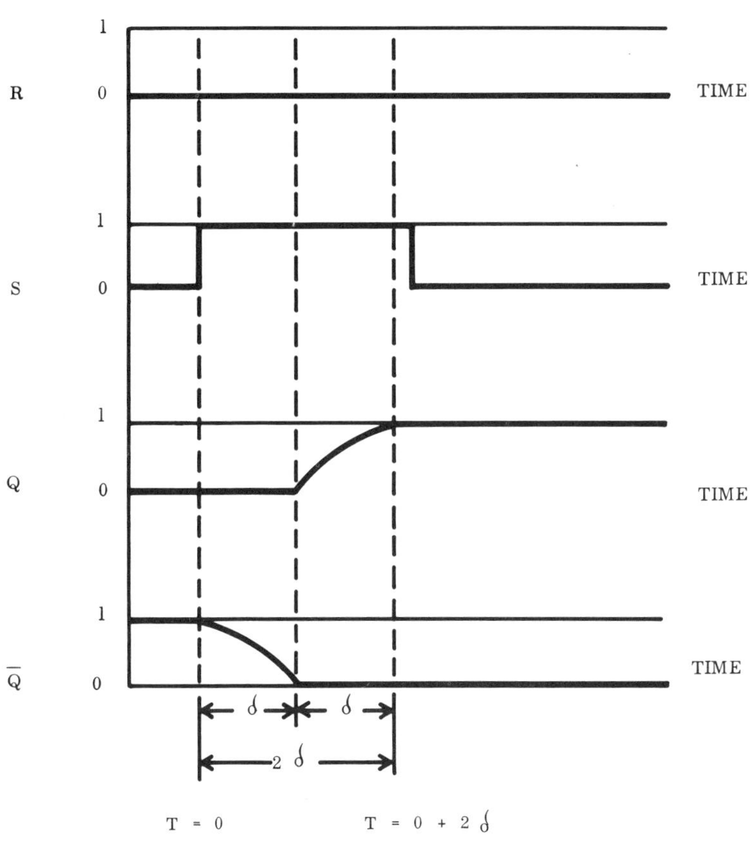

Figure 14–4

differ merely in the methods used to toggle them (or to change from the set to the reset state). All of them are similar in that they have two output lines which are always the complement of each other except during the brief time periods involved in actual toggling.

THE T OR TRIGGERED FLIP FLOP

A type T flip flop differs from a type RS in that it has only 1 input line labeled T. While an RS flip flop can be toggled by either a pulse or steady state signal on the S or R line, a type T is always toggled by a pulse on the T line. Figure 14–5 shows the logic symbols for both an RS and a type T flip flop.

An incoming pulse on line T will toggle the outputs to the opposite state whether the device was in the set or reset condition when the pulse arrived; hence a type T flip flop is also called a complementing flip flop.

As will be shown in the next chapter, type T flip flops are often used in ripple counters, and in writing the timing diagrams for such devices it is important to know when a flip flop will toggle with respect to an incoming pulse. A type T flip flop will toggle either on the positive going edge of a pulse (the leading edge in positive logic) or the negative going edge of a pulse (the trailing edge in positive logic) but never both. Which direction a particular device triggers on must be known. This information is obtained from the manufacturer's spec sheets.

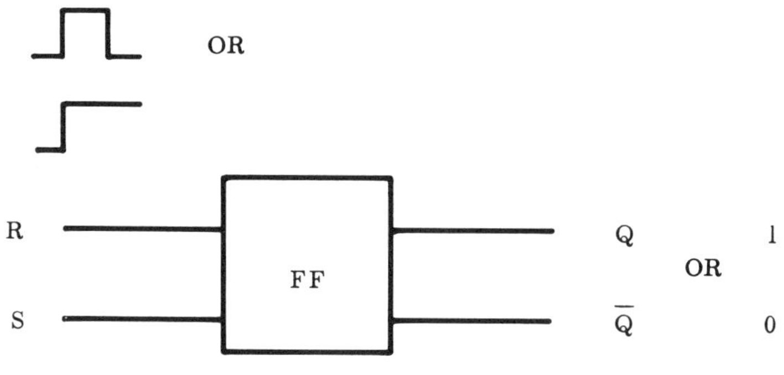

TYPE RS FLIP FLOP

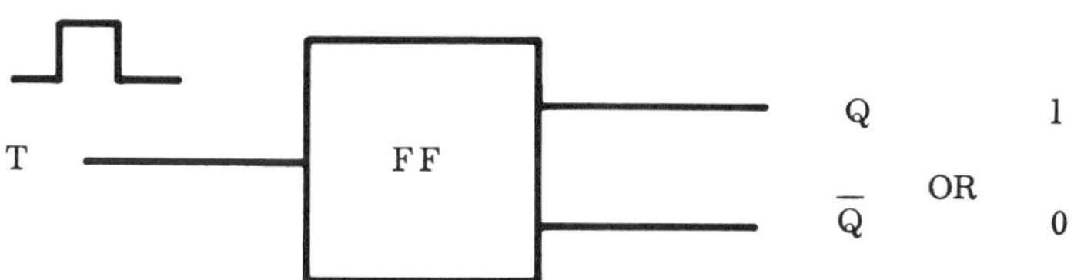

TYPE T FLIP FLOP

Figure 14–5

The Type RST or Delayed Flip Flop

An RS flip flop will toggle on either a steady state or a pulsed input. A type T flip flop requires a pulse to toggle it. A type RST flip flop is designed to be operated when a steady state set or clear (reset) signal coexists with a triggering pulse. Thus, a set or reset signal on the input will do nothing until the triggering pulse arrives. A triggering pulse in the absence of a 1 on either the R or S line will do nothing. For this reason a type RST flip flop is often called a synchronous flip flop; i.e., the trigger pulse and the set or clear signal must coexist, or be synchronous. This is a useful device for sequential operations when it is desired to set up conditions for a subsequent step in advance and use a clock pulse to control the precise time the new conditions go into effect.

Figure 14–6(a) shows how a type RST flip flop is represented on a logic diagram. Figure 14–6(b) shows how such a flip flop can be implemented with nor gates. If it was desired to use nand gates instead, all that need be remembered is that the nand and nor functions are duals, and the nand gate type RST flip flop of Figure 14–6(c) can be drawn directly from the nor gates of Figure 14–6(b) by simply inverting all variables and replacing each nor gate with a nand gate.

As a practical matter, the reader will never make a flip flop up out of gates except in an emergency since they are commercially available as

S
CP OR T
R
FF
Q
Q̄
1
OR
0
A
R
T
S
R
S
R
Q
S
Q̄
Q
Q̄
BASIC RS FLIP FLOP IN NOR LOGIC
B
R
T
S
R
S
R̄
S̄
Q̄
Q
Q̄
Q
BASIC RS FLIP FLOP IN NAND LOGIC
C
TYPE RST FLIP FLOP

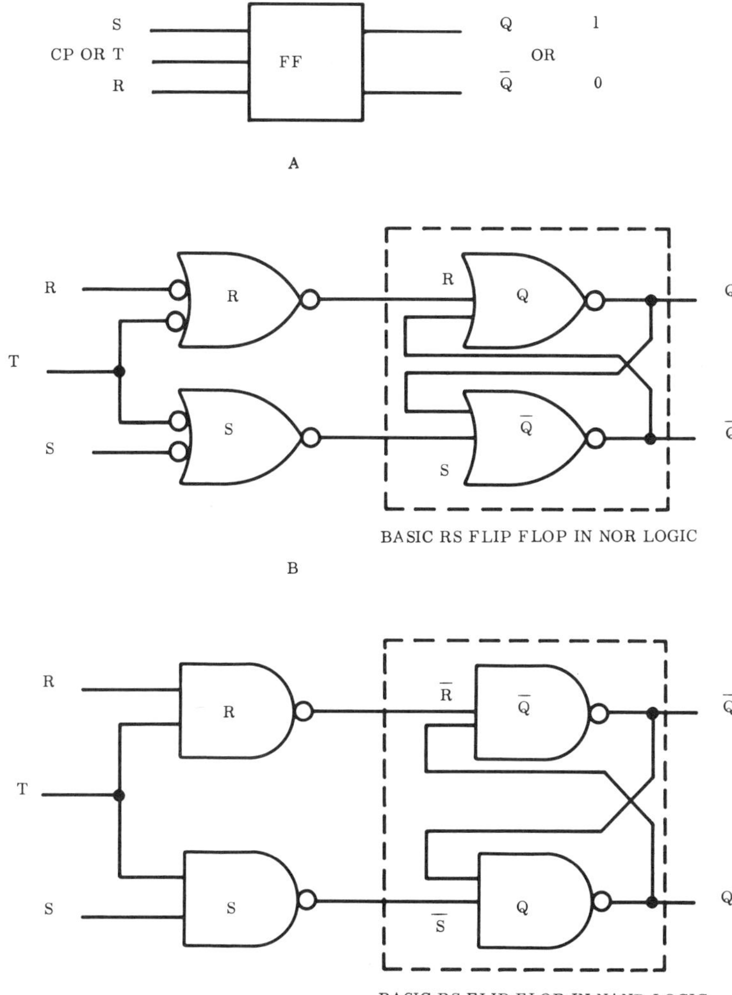

Figure 14–6

logic packages. However, knowing how they work enables one to do more with whatever logic modules are available.

In Figure 14–6(b) the reader will recognize the basic RS flip flop whose action has been described previously. What has been done is to add a stage in front of this consisting of two nor gates with their inputs inverted. The action of this total system will be made clear by considering the effect of nor gate R associated with reset pulse R. To make the flip flop clear or reset, it is obvious that the output of this gate to the basic RS flip flop must be a 1. But the only way to get a 1 out of nor gate R is for the output of the basic *or* gate (to the left of the output negation symbol) to be 0. This in turn requires that both inputs be 0. Since each input is negated, this condition can only obtain when both lines R and T have a 1 on them, QED.

The exact same reasoning can be used to show that the set nor gate, S, will only apply a 1 to the set line of the basic RS flip flop when both lines T and S have a 1 on them.

In Figure 14–6(c) it can be seen that the conversion of the basic RS flip flop to nand logic results in the requirement of a 0 level signal on the set or reset lines to toggle the device. Here the action of gates R or S are simpler to visualize if both lines R and T have a 1 on them. Then the output of basic *and* gate R will be 1. When this is then inverted, the 0 level needed to toggle the basic RS flip flop is obtained.

It is important to realize that a type RST flip flop is really one combining the properties of an RS and a T type, and as in the case of the former device a 1 is never permitted on both lines R and S at the same time. This should be apparent from a study of Figure 14–6. It should also be apparent from Figure 14–6 that, since there is now an additional stage used, the total toggle time required will be 3δ instead of 2δ as in a plain RS flip flop.

THE J-K FLIP FLOPS

A J-K flip flop is basically an RS flip flop with one added feature. The J line acts as a set or S line, and the K line acts as an R or clear line. The added feature is the fact that, unlike the RS flip flop, the J-K can have both the J and the K line at the 1 level at the same time. When this condition occurs, the flip flop will toggle or complement whatever condition previously existed. This is referred to as the J-K mode of operation, and it explains why this device is the most commonly used flip flop—it can do everything that an RS flip flop can do and then some. There are many specific types of J-K flip flops that combine desirable features of the other types of flip flops mentioned and some special ones of their own. Figure 14–7(a) shows the logic symbol for the basic J-K flip flop, Figure 14–7(b) shows how this device can be made from nand gates and time delays, and Figure 14–7(c) shows how this configuration is customarily represented with the time delays omitted

J
K
FF
Q
Q̄
OR
1
0
A
J
K
J
K
Q
Q̄
Q
Q̄
B
J
K
J
K
Q
Q̄
Q
Q̄
C
BASIC RS FLIP FLOP
IN NAND FORM WITH
THE 2 FEEDBACK LINES
BROUGHT OUT
BASIC J-K FLIP FLOP

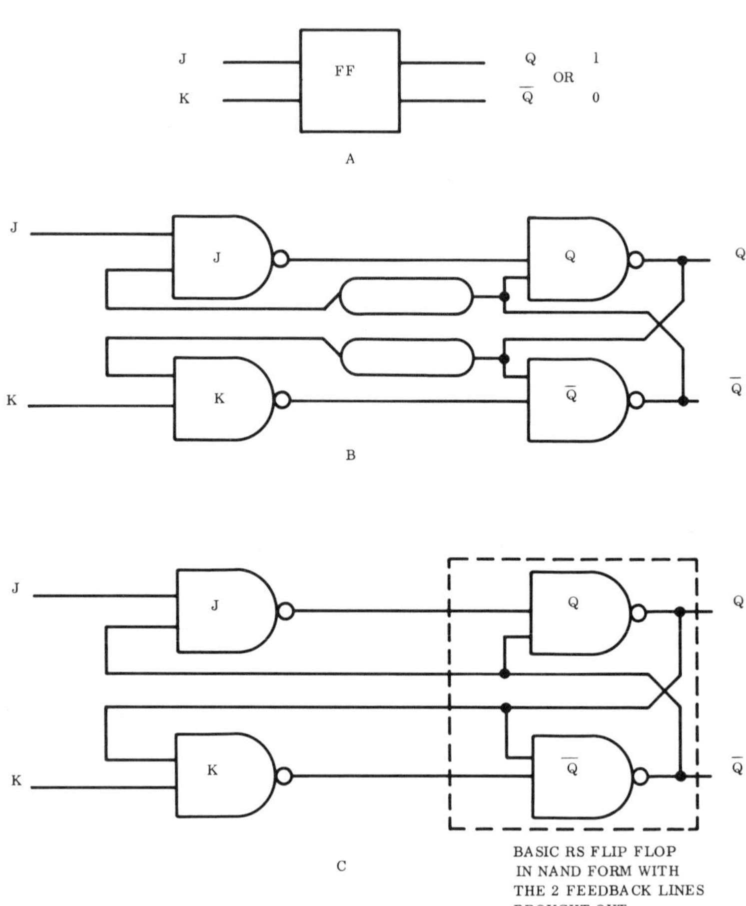

Figure 14–7

for the sake of simplicity. Even though the time delays are not always shown, they are vital to prevent the erratic operation of the system in the J-K mode.

The reader would be well advised to accept the operation of this device on faith, and then he can go on to examine some useful variations of the basic configuration of Figure 14–7. If he chooses to do so, however, he can consider the device of Figure 14–7(b) to be in either the set or reset state and trace the action through step by step when 1's are simultaneously applied on the J and K lines. This is best done by setting up a timing diagram like the one in Figure 14–4 where the inputs and outputs of each gate are represented at the 1 or 0 level as a function of time and the time sequence is worked out step by step.

There is one limitation on the use of the basic J-K flip flop. It cannot be used with steady state input signals, but must be driven by pulses. Furthermore the pulses require the proper pulse width; i.e., they must be above a certain minimum in duration. This value is given by the manufacturer of commercial modules and results from consideration of the timing diagrams of these devices.

Clocked J-K Flip Flops

Figure 14–8 shows how the basic J-K flip flop of Figure 14–7(c) can be modified by the use of three-input nand gates to provide a synchronous mode of

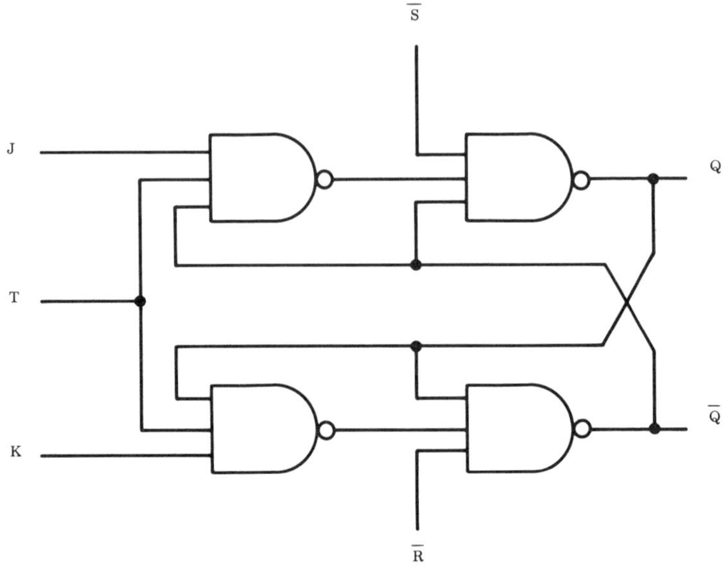

CLOCKED OR SYNCRONOUS J-K FLIP FLOP

Figure 14–8

operation similar to an RST flip flop wherein the J and K lines are only effective when a clock or synchronizing pulse is present on line T.

Since three-input nand gates are used, a $\overline{S}$ and $\overline{R}$ line is provided in the second stage which permits this unit to be operated in the RS mode with steady state signals. Note also that the RS mode here does not depend on the presence of a clock pulse as does the J-K mode. If working with 0 set or reset signals causes confusion, simply insert inverters in the $\overline{S}$ and $\overline{R}$ lines or convert to nor logic.

Multiple J-K Flip Flops

As Figure 14–9 shows, a multiple J-K flip flop is merely a clocked J-K flip flop with multiple nand gates used for the input stage gates. Since this unit can be purchased as a logic package, it will often save additional gates in a final system. If, however, all of the inputs are not needed, all that need be done is to parallel the unused inputs with an input being used. This is a general technique to be used any time an *and* or nand gate has more inputs than are needed. Thus a five input *and* gate can be reduced to a two input gate by connecting four input leads together.

Master — Slave or Dual Ranked J-K Flip Flops

A dual ranked J-K flip flop consists of two basic RS flip flops cascaded as shown in Figure 14–10; the inputs of each are controlled by a pair of *and* gates. This system has two advantages. First it produces the J-K mode of operation without the need of internal time delays. Second, from the point of view of the beginner, the operation of the dual ranked J-K flip flop is easier to follow when drawn in the conventional manner of Figure 14–10.

As can be seen from Figure 14–10, the clock pulse is fed directly to the two *and* gates controlling the master flip flop and is inverted before being fed into the *and* gates controlling the slave or output flip flop. For this reason this flip flop is actuated on

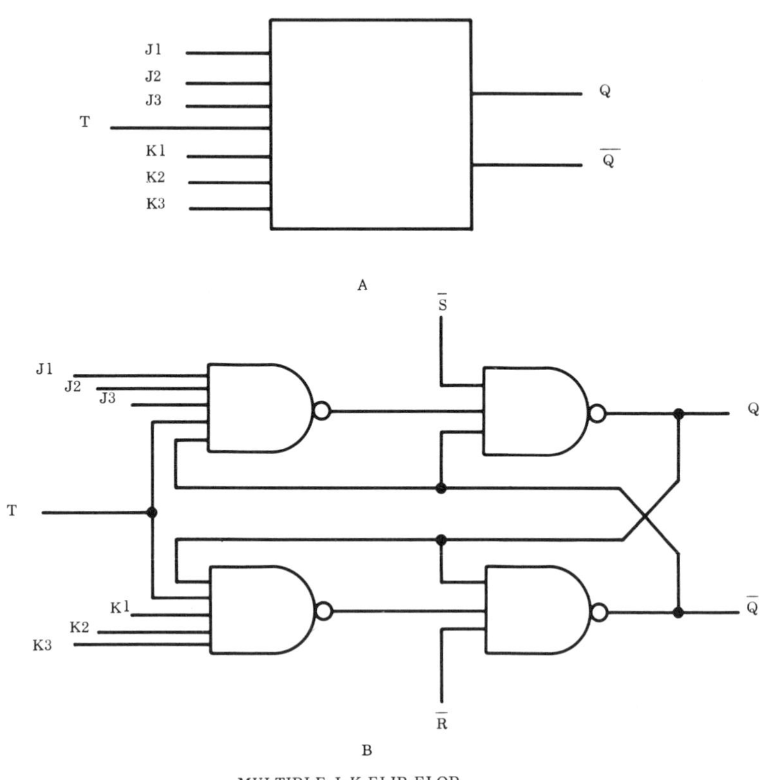

MULTIPLE J-K FLIP FLOP

Figure 14-9

both edges of the clock pulse. Thus, the leading edge of the clock pulse is a 1, and it therefore puts a 0 on the output stage *and* gates disabling the slave flip flop and holding it in its present state while the master flip flop is being toggled. On the decaying edge of the pulse, a 0 is put on the master flip flop *and* gates, holding this flip flop in its new state while its output is used to toggle the slave flip flop whose *and* gates now get a 1 from the clock pulse line. It will be noticed that feeding the outputs of each FF to the inputs of the *and* gates of the other flip flop prevents either pair of *and* gates associated with the same flip flop from ever having 1 outputs at the same time.

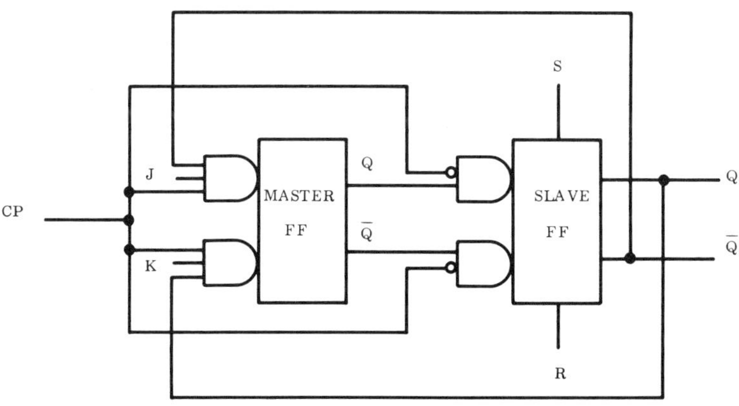

DUAL RANKED FLIP FLOP

Figure 14–10

The total time for a change in state will be equal to the clock pulse width plus 2δ for a perfectly shaped pulse, but since the latter is small in comparison to the former and pulses are never perfectly square it will be approximately equal to the pulse width. To get the maximum possible toggling speed, the pulse width should be equal to about 4δ, but this will rarely be a problem in experimental apparatus design where the slowest flip flops will be adequate for most applications.

If the reader is still on board at this point, he now knows all he will ever need to know about basic logic devices. What remains to be shown in the next chapter is how flip flops can be utilized to create useful devices such as counters and shift registers. Then the reader will be ready to understand how these logic devices, together with certain nonlogic devices, can be used to solve a whole variety of equipment design problems easily and economically.

Chapter 15
Counters and Shift Registers

The flip flop, a device that will remain in either of two possible states until toggled by an incoming signal, is ideally suited to use as a memory element in a binary system. In this chapter we will consider how these memory devices are combined into larger subsystems, called counters or shift registers, which have many practical applications in logic systems.

Figure 15–1(a) shows three type T flip flops connected to form a ripple counter which will count up from 0 to 7 and keep repeating this cycle. The operation of this ripple counter can be followed from the timing diagram shown in Figure 15–2.

As can be seen from Figure 15–1(a), the $\overline{Q}$ line of each flip flop is used to feed the T line of the next flip flop. The marks on the positive going edge of the pulses shown in the timing diagram (Figure 15–2) indicate that this is the pulse edge that triggers the next flip flop into toggling.

A study of the timing diagram of Figure 15–2 reveals an important use of counters. It will be

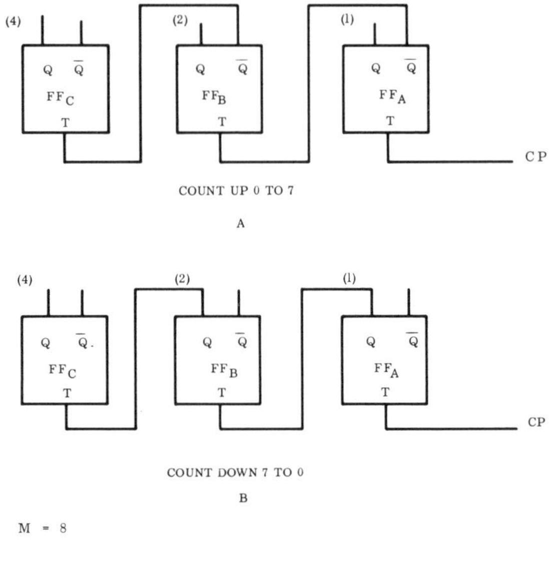

Figure 15-1

noticed that the output of flip flop A has $\frac{1}{2}$ the frequency of the clock pulse, the output of flip flop B has $\frac{1}{2}$ the frequency of flip flop A, etc. Hence, a counter can function as a frequency divider. Each additional stage or flip flop in the counter will reduce the output frequency by $\frac{1}{2}$. Hence in the three stage counter of Figure 15-1, the final output frequency of flip flop C will be $\frac{1}{8}$ of the input clock pulse frequency. The intermediate output points, i.e., those of flip flop B or A, will yield outputs of $\frac{1}{4}$ and $\frac{1}{2}$ the clock input frequency respectively.

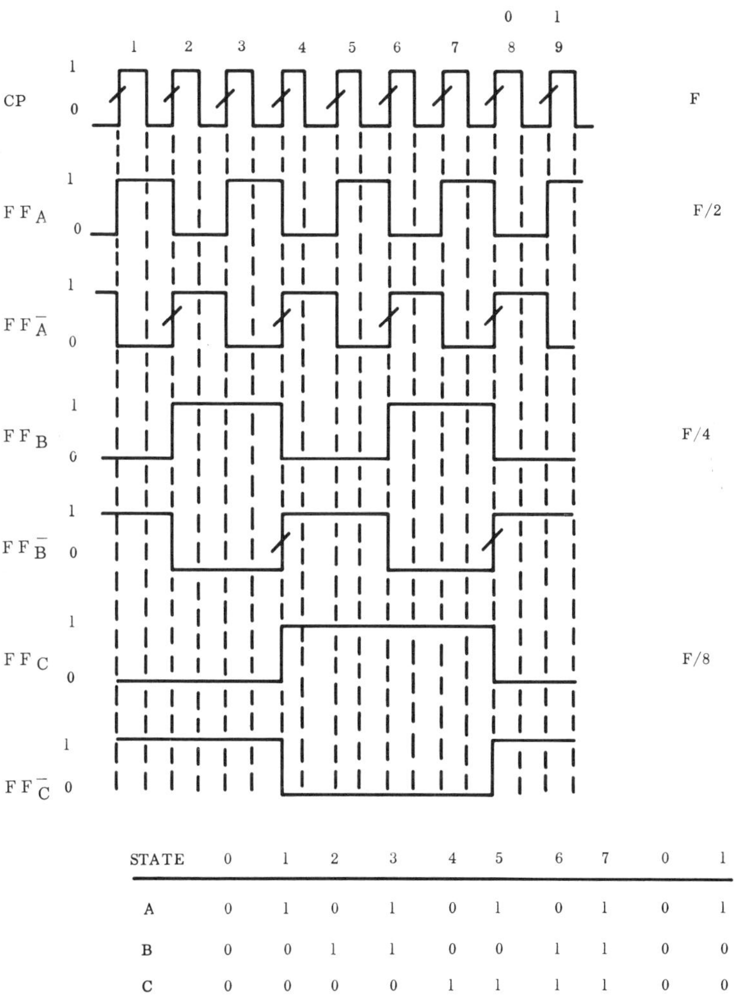

STATE	0	1	2	3	4	5	6	7	0	1
A	0	1	0	1	0	1	0	1	0	1
B	0	0	1	1	0	0	1	1	0	0
C	0	0	0	0	1	1	1	1	0	0

TIMING DIAGRAM OF COUNT UP RIPPLE COUNTER OF FIGURE 15-1A

(TIME DELAYS PER FLIP FLOP OMITTED TO SIMPLIFY)

Figure 15-2

If the Q lines of each flip flop in the counter are properly weighted, i.e., FF $A = 1$. FF $B = 2$ and FF $C = 4$, then these three lines will represent the state of the count directly in the form of a three bit binary number as shown in the output state diagram of Figure 15-2.

In the operation of this counter, the signal must ripple through each of the flip flops successively, and hence the name ripple counter. If each flip flop has a propagation or transit time delay of 2δ, then it follows that the total time delay through the counter will be a maximum of $N \times 2\delta$, where N is the number of flip flops. Not so obvious is the fact that each change in count of a ripple counter does not take an equal time to occur. For example, in going from state 6 to state 7 in the output state diagram of Figure 15-2 only one flip flop, A, has to toggle, while in going from state 7 to state 0 the signal must ripple through all three flip flops. Hence, ripple counters are slow and have variable operating times.

The reader will also observe that in Figure 15-1(a) the clock pulse or signal is shown as traveling from right to left across the diagram; this is contrary to the usual convention for signal flow. The reason for this is that the first flip flop, A, represents the least significant bit (LSB) in the binary number representing the count, and the number writing convention of having the least significant digit on the right takes precedence over the signal flow convention.

The true power of the counter as a control or

programing device can be appreciated by considering the nature of the incoming pulses. If as shown in Figure 15–2 these are clock pulses coming from an accurate frequency source or oscillator, the counter is in effect a clock and can be used to initiate or terminate events at precise time intervals. If on the other hand the incoming pulses are generated nontemporally (for example, as a result of the operation of some manipulanda), the counter is then an event counter and can be used to initiate or terminate events as a function of other events as opposed to time. Thus, the same basic device can be used to generate either interval or ratio schedules in a Skinner box situation.

Figure 15–1(b) shows how the same three flip flops can be connected to produce a counter that counts down from 7 to 0. The only difference between Figures 15–1(a) and (b) is that in (b) the Q lines, instead of the $\overline{Q}$ lines, are used to drive the next stage. It is left as an exercise for the reader to work out the timing diagram for this count down counter and its output state table. The only point that the reader must remember in doing this is that it is assumed that the flip flops used toggle on the positive going edge of the pulse.

The modulus (M) of a counter is the number of pulses that it will count before recycling and starting over at 0. For a ripple counter $M = 2^N$, where $N =$ the number of flip flops used. Thus for the three flip flop counter of Figure 15–1, $M = 2^3 = 8$ and there are 8 states counted before the counter repeats. With four flip flops, the counter would count 16 different states (from 0 to 15), etc.

While it is not possible to count a number higher than the modulus of a counter, it is possible through logic to cut the count short or recycle before reaching the full count that could be obtained. Hence, a shortened modulus counter could be used to limit the count to any number less than the modulus. The most common example of a shortened modulus counter is a decimal counter where it is desired to limit the count to numbers from 0 to 9. To do this, we must start out with a counter having a modulus of at least 10. Hence by the formula, $M = 2^N$, it is apparent that a basic counter with a modulus of 16, or four flip flops, is needed. More flip flops could be used, but since the count is to be cut short there is no point in doing so.

Figure 15–3 shows a logic diagram to accomplish this reduced modulus operation. It will be noted that the output lines of the counter are all fed into the logic gate so that it can sense the state of the count.

What is needed is for the logic gate to generate a 1 level output when the counter momentarily enters state 10. This output is then used to reset the flip flops in the counter putting it back in the 0 count position where the next incoming pulse will start the count over. This will occur so quickly that the counter will for all practical purposes never record an output in state 10. In order to prevent undesirable transient conditions caused by unequal reset

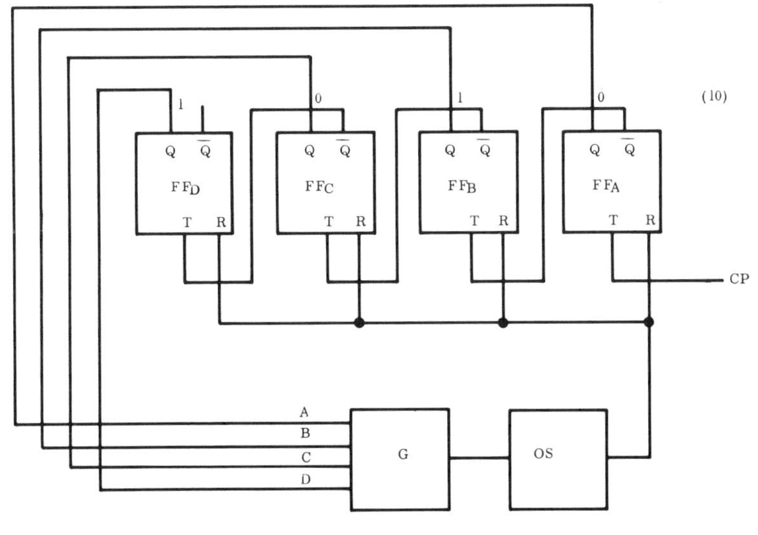

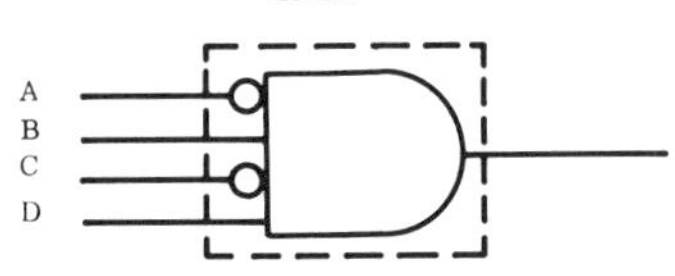

GATE

SHORTENED MODULUS DECIMAL COUNTER

Figure 15–3

times of the different flip flops in the counter, a pulse stretching device is needed on the gate output to assure that all flip flops will have reset before the reset pulse is removed. A one shot multivibrator (Described in Chapter 12) used as a pulse stretcher will accomplish this end.

The reader is now well prepared to design the

logic required for the gate function of Figure 15–3. Treat the Q lines of the four flip flops as inputs to the gate, write out the standard basis, and fill out the designation number of the required function bit by bit. With a little experience these formal steps will not be needed except in fairly complicated situations. In this case, for example, it is clear that what is wanted is a 1 level output clear signal when the weighted input lines represent a binary number 10. In this case, since binary 10 is written 1010, then $A = 0$, $B = 1$, $C = 0$, and $D = 1$. Thus, all that is needed for gate G is a four-input *and* gate to generate the function $\overline{A} \cdot B \cdot \overline{C} \cdot D$, as shown in Figure 15–3.

The reader has probably noticed that binary numbers tend to be much longer than corresponding decimal numbers. If a large decimal number is converted into a binary number, the binary number tends to become unwieldly, and more important the notation tends to become confusing. Therefore a method of treatment called binary coded decimal (BCD) has come into use. For example, in converting the decimal number 263 into BCD what is done is to write the binary number for each digit of the decimal number as follows rather than to express 263 into a binary number directly; i.e.,

BCD	2	6	3
	010	110	011
Binary	263		
	100000111		

This technique of using binary coded decimal numbers is often used in counters. This is done by using a separate counter for each position in the decimal number. Thus, Figure 15–4 shows a device for counting from 0 to 99 which is made by cascading the output of a decimal counter counting from 0 to 9 or units into a decimal counter which is now counting by 10's. Such a device is called a decade counter. It will be noted that by adding an additional identical decimal counter the device would count to 999 with the additional counter representing 100's. The gating pulse used to reset the first decimal counter is used to drive the next one at the conclusion of the first counter's full count, and so on.

All of the counters described so far are continuous counters. In other words, after the full count has been obtained the next pulse will set the counter to 0, and it will start to count again. In some situations it might be desired to go through a full count and then stop until the counter is manu-

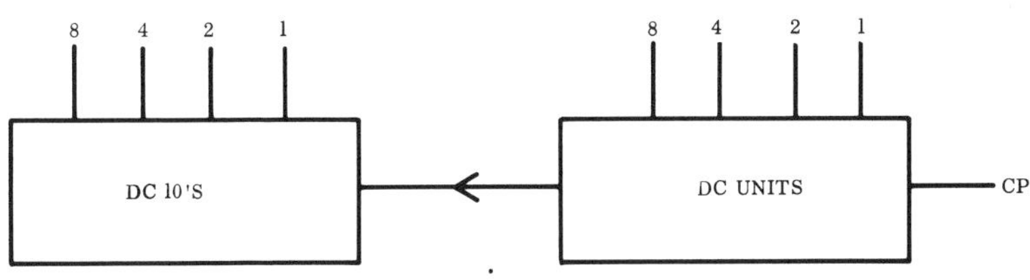

Figure 15–4

8
4
2
1
Q   Q̄
FF_D
T   R
Q   Q̄
FF_C
T   R
Q   Q̄
FF_B
T   R
Q   Q̄
FF_A
T   R
G
TD
DECIMAL COUNTER
STOP PULSE
START PULSE
R   Q
CONTROL
S   FF   Q̄
CP
CYCLE COUNTER

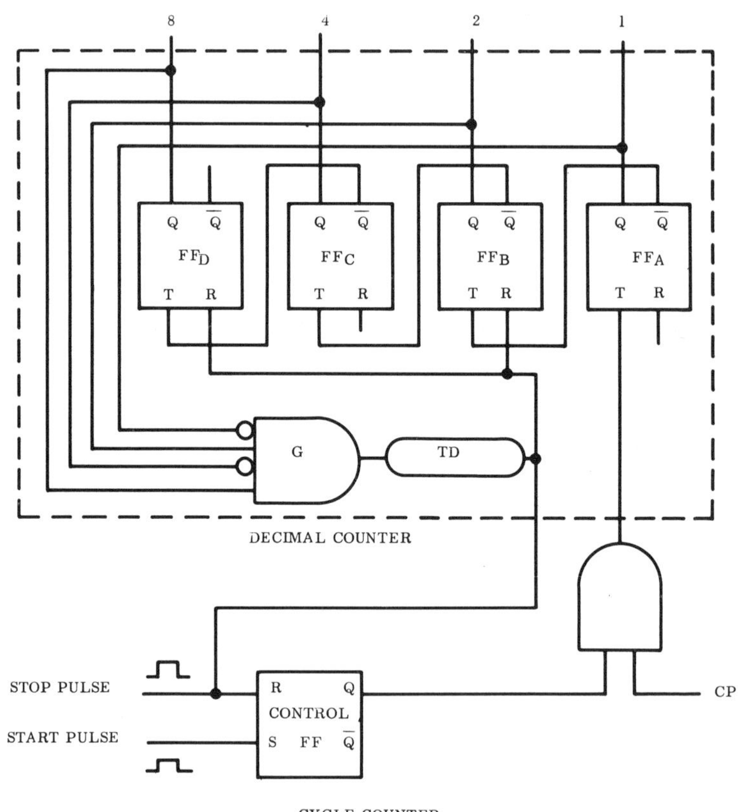

Figure 15–5

ally reset. Such a counter, which will only count through one cycle unless reset, is called a cycle counter. Such a device can be readily created by the logic control illustrated in Figure 15–5; this device uses an additional flip flop to control the cycle.

As can be seen from Figure 15–5, the counting is started when a start pulse is applied to the set input of the control flip flop. This puts a 1 on the input of the *and* gate and holds it there as long as the control flip flop is not reset. Thus each incoming clock pulse is passed through the gate and counted. When the decimal counter has completed one counting cycle, the same gating logic used to cut the counting modulus short provides a 1 level signal to the reset terminal of the control flip flop and toggles it so that now there is a 0 level signal fed to the *and* gate. This prevents the passage of clock pulses until the cycle is started again by the application of another start pulse. It should be noted that this method of control can be used with any counter or combination of counters. If the basic counter is not a shortened modulus type then, of course, the logic for the generation of the stop pulse at the appropriate time would have to be added externally, but this should present no problem.

Until this point, the discussion has dealt exclusively with ripple counters. These have been dealt with first because they are simple to design and involve trivial logic circuits. While they will be adequate for most laboratory apparatus situations, they suffer from the problem of variable delay times or transients. The reader should be aware that there are other types of counters, called parallel counters, which eliminate these problems, although they are somewhat more complex to design. Figure 15–6 shows three type T flip flops connected as a parallel counter.

Note that in the parallel counter the clock pulse is fed simultaneously to all of the flip flops and changes in state occur at the same time. The signal, thus, does not have to ripple through from stage to

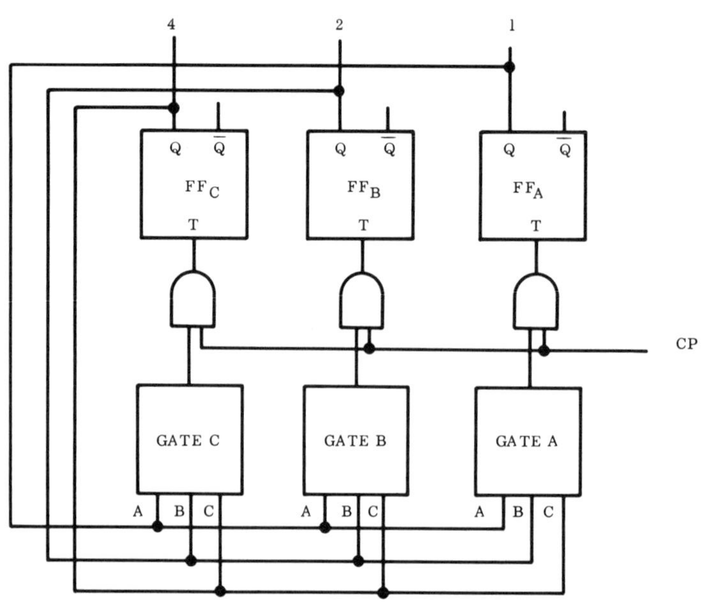

PARALLEL COUNTER

Figure 15–6

stage. The toggle time is thus constant for all counts, and the delay time is much less than in a ripple counter. However, whether or not an individual flip flop is to change state on a particular clock pulse must be determined by an individual logic circuit or gate for each flip flop. It can be seen from Figure 15–6 that all of the output lines are used as inputs for the control gates associated with each flip flop. It can also be seen that to get a particular flip flop to change state on a clock pulse the output of the logic gate associated with that flip flop must put a 1 level signal on the associated *and* gate. Therefore, the design of these logic gates involves nothing more than treating the counter flip flop output (Q_A, Q_B, and Q_C) as inputs to the gates and writing them in the standard basis format. Then under each column it is simply necessary to write whether the output of the logic gate should be a 1 or a 0 for that particular input state. This is determined by whether the flip flop is to toggle or not on the next clock pulse. This must be done for each of the three gate functions involved. To illustrate this let us design a straightforward count up counter from the configuration of Figure 15–6. Since there are three flip flops, a modulus 8 counter, or a device which can be made to count up from 0 to 7, results. The truth table is shown in Table 15–1.

Whether a 1 or a 0 should be written for each gate in each column was determined by considering whether or not the associated flip flop had to toggle in going to the next count. For example, in going from state 2 to state 3:

State	2	3		2
Q_A	0	1	FF$_A$ toggles	GA 1
Q_B	1	1	FF$_B$ doesn't toggle	GB 0
Q_C	0	0	FF$_C$ doesn't toggle	GC 0
GA	1			
GB	0			
GC	0			

Since a 1 level output is the only way the flip flop associated with a gate can be made to toggle, simply write a 1 in the column under input state 2 for any gate controlling a flip flop which must change state and a 0 for any flip flop gate that must retain the same state on the next count.

Thus, designation numbers for all of the re-

Table 15–1

Inputs	Weights	Decimal Equivalent of Input State							
		0	1	2	3	4	5	6	7
Q_A	1	0	1	0	1	0	1	0	1
Q_B	2	0	0	1	1	0	0	1	1
Q_C	4	0	0	0	0	1	1	1	1

Outputs		Decimal Equivalent of Next Output State							
		1	2	3	4	5	6	7	0
G_A	1	1	1	1	1	1	1	1	1
G_B	2	0	1	0	1	1	0	0	1
G_C	4	0	0	0	1	0	0	0	1

quired gate functions are obtained, and the design of this counter becomes a routine matter of simplifying the logic and drawing the final flow diagram.

The same logic gates could be used to produce a shortened modulus counter. For example, the truth table could be written so that when count 5 occurred the next pulse would put the counter back in state 0 and resume the cycle from that point. The only thing that would change is the logic requirements for the control gates. Thus, this basic configuration can be used to count up or down and to make shortened modulus and decimal counters. Like ripple counters, basic parallel counters can be combined into decade counters or made into a cycle counter.

One additional thing that a parallel counter can do simply that a ripple counter cannot is to count any sequence of numbers less than its modulus in any order. For example, the sequence 3, 2, 5, 1 could be counted in the order given by the selection of the proper logic for the gates shown in Figure 15-6.

To design such a counter simply write out the counting sequence desired and under each number abstract from the standard basis the input states corresponding to it as follows:

	3	2	5	1	(3)
Q_A	1	0	1	1	1
Q_B	1	1	1	0	1
Q_C	0	0	1	0	0

Then the table can be completed by simply considering which flip flop must toggle in going from one count to the next as follows:

	3	2	5	1	(3)
Q_A	1	0	1	1	1
Q_B	1	1	1	0	1
Q_C	0	0	1	0	0
G_A	1	1	0	0	0
G_B	0	0	1	1	1
G_C	0	1	1	1	0

It is essential for the reader to realize that the above diagram has not given us a designation number for the gate output functions since the inputs were not written in the standard basis. However, a logic diagram for each gate can be written directly from this table if it is realized that it defines which of the eight possible combinations of input states are required for a 0 or 1 output level from each gate. Hence, this counter could be implemented directly using the logic diagram of Figure 15–7.

Reading directly from our "truth table," the "go" conditions for a 1 output on each of the three gates can be seen to be:

	Gate A	Gate B	Gate C
Go conditions	$A \cdot B \cdot \overline{C}$	$A \cdot B \cdot C$	$\overline{A} \cdot B \cdot \overline{C}$
	$\overline{A} \cdot B \cdot C$	$A \cdot \overline{B} \cdot \overline{C}$	$A \cdot B \cdot C$
		$A \cdot B \cdot \overline{C}$	$A \cdot \overline{B} \cdot \overline{C}$

4
2
1
Q Q̄
Q Q̄
Q Q̄
FF C
FF B
FF A
T
T
T
CP
GATE C
GATE B
GATE A
ABC̄
ĀBC̄
ABC
AB̄C̄

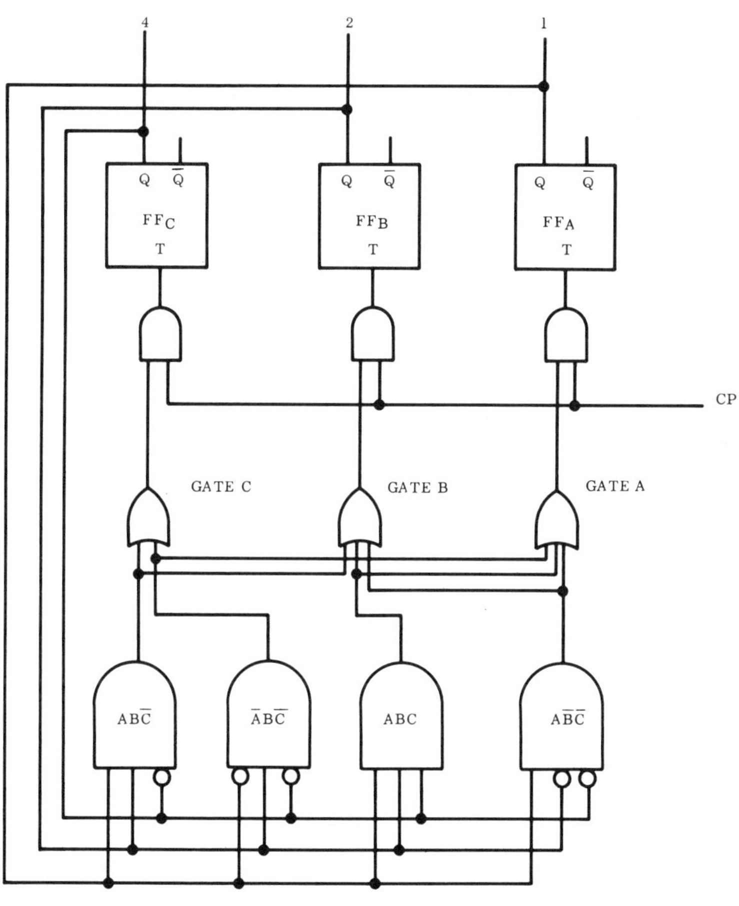

Figure 15–7

All other input conditions are "no go" conditions that must produce a 0 output from these gates.

Before writing out the logic diagram in the form of eight *and* gates, notice that there are only four different *and* gates represented, each being used twice. Thus, the logic could be implemented using only four 3-input *and* gates. However, let us consider if the *and* gates used in each function gate can be further simplified by factoring.

Thus for Gate A:

$$(A \cdot B \cdot \overline{C}) + (\overline{A} \cdot B \cdot \overline{C}) = B \cdot \overline{C}(A + \overline{A}) = B \cdot \overline{C}$$

For Gate B:

$$(A \cdot B \cdot C) + (A \cdot \overline{B} \cdot \overline{C}) + (A \cdot B \cdot \overline{C})$$
$$= A \cdot B(C + \overline{C}) + (A \cdot \overline{B} \cdot \overline{C})$$
$$= A \cdot B + A \cdot \overline{B} \cdot \overline{C}$$

For Gate C:

$$(\overline{A} \cdot B \cdot \overline{C}) + (A \cdot B \cdot C) + (A \cdot \overline{B} \cdot \overline{C})$$
$$= \overline{A} \cdot B \cdot \overline{C} + A(\overline{B} \cdot \overline{C} + B \cdot C)$$

Note that the last term does not reduce to A because the expression $\overline{B} \cdot \overline{C} \neq \overline{B \cdot C}$. Thus, we would end up with two different 2-input *and* gates and three different 3-input *and* gates for the logic diagram of Figure 15–7. Depending on the kind of hardware being used one or the other way might be more convenient, but we have chosen to use four 3-input *and* gates.

While the counters described above will be the most useful memory devices for the apparatus de-

LSB
SEQUENTIAL
BINARY
INPUT
STAGE
D
C
B
A
Q
S
T
R
Q̄
CP
CP 0   0   0   0   0   1011
CP 1   0   0   0   1   -011
CP 2   0   0   1   0   --11
CP 3   0   1   0   1   ---1
CP 4   1   0   1   1   ----
SHIFT REGISTER

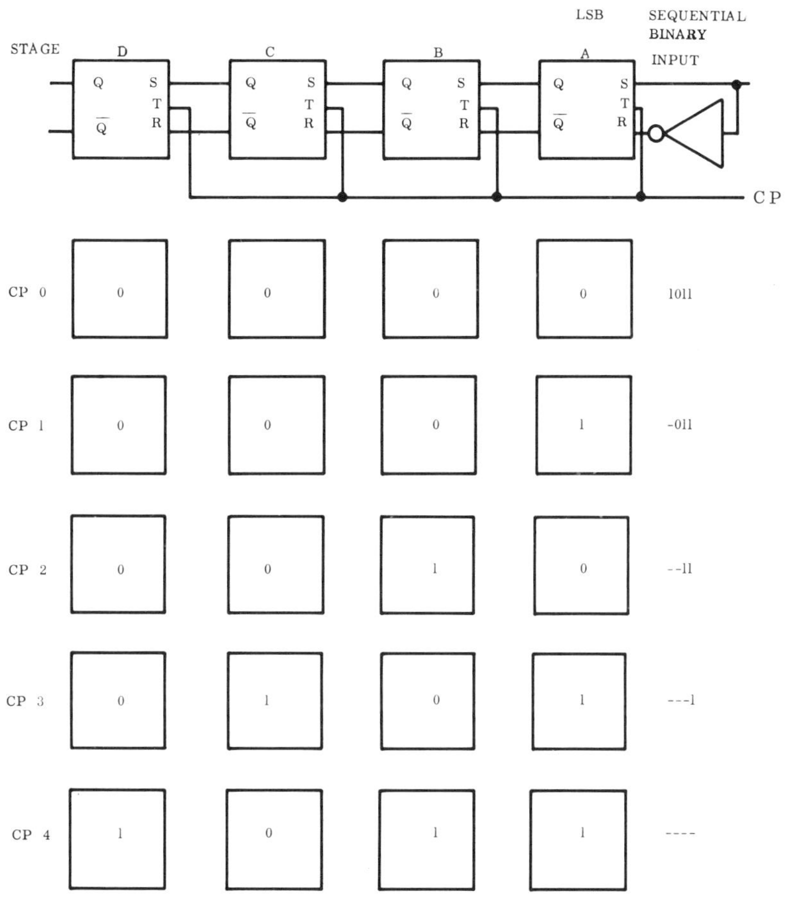

Figure 15–8

signer, there is another type of memory device that will be mentioned briefly at this point. This device is called a shift register, and Figure 15–8 shows four flip flops connected to form one.

Like counters, shift registers can be purchased as completely integrated circuit packages, but they can also be made as shown from basic flip flops (which in turn can be made from basic nor or nand gates).

A shift register gets its name from the fact that with each incoming pulse the 0 or 1 stored in each flip flop is shifted along to the next flip flop in the chain. As can be seen in Figure 15–8, the sequential series of 1's and 0's fed into the register are brought in on one line, and the clocking pulse is brought in on another. Unlike a counter, the shift register does not respond to or count the incoming clock pulses. Its function is simply to step the memory signals along. As in the case of a counter, however, this stepping pulse can come from a clock or occur randomly as a result of the operation of manipulanda.

Chapter 16
Hardware Systems

After a logic system has been designed to solve a specific problem, it is necessary to implement this system in terms of practical hardware. There are several ways of implementation possible for the same paper design.

One approach is for the logic designer to change hats and become an electronic designer. He could sit down and design transistorized gate circuits, build them, and then use these to implement his logic diagram. He might also buy gates that someone else has designed and built commercially, saving himself this step. The fact is that no one would do either except as an exercise, for the day has long since past where anyone would consider building logic gates out of standard electronic components like transistors, resistors, etc.

Techniques have now been developed for the building of what are called integrated circuits, or μ logic packages. As a result of these techniques, several basic gates can be purchased commercially for a few cents in a package the size of a pea. It is from these basic building blocks that the final logic system will ultimately be built.

The manufacturers of these integrated circuits (IC's) have come out with a series of compatible gates and devices that can be put together into any logic configuration. By compatible it is meant that the 1 and 0 voltage levels for all of these packages will be the same and the supply voltage needed to operate these gates (which is never shown on any logic diagram) will be the same. Besides basic nor or nand gates, larger subsystems (such as counters, shift registers, etc.) can also be purchased in these compatible systems. The very first thing that the beginning logic designer should do is to request catalogues from a few manufacturers of logic modules. These catalogues will provide a wealth of information about the gates available for a system and their characteristics, e.g., 0 and 1 voltage levels, supply voltage requirements, transit times, etc. For each package the manufacturer will usually show the logic diagram for the package and the pinning diagram showing where all the inputs, outputs, and supply voltages must be connected. Often the equivalent electronic schematic of the device will be given which may frighten the non-electronic user. But don't worry, the electronic schematic is totally irrelevant as far as the use of the device is concerned.

For each gate, the manufacturer will also give values for what is called the unit load of input lines and the fanout of output lines. These terms are very important, so they will be considered now.

Basically a gate is an electronic circuit, although it has been considered here on a functional basis rather than in terms of the specific circuits used. Therefore, each input line represents some electrical impedance which it presents to the circuit driving it. It will, therefore, draw some current that the driving device must be capable of supplying, and it will dissipate some energy in the form of heat. Rather than have logic designers turn into part time electrical engineers, the manufacturers have designated the term unit load to represent a given power requirement to drive a gate. On the output end of the gate, the term "fanout" refers to the number of unit loads a gate is capable of driving. For example, if the *or* gates in a system have inputs of 3 unit loads and the *and* gates have a fanout of 10 then the logic designer knows that one *and* gate can be used to drive up to three *or* gates. He doesn't have to be concerned with how much driving power must be supplied to these *or* gates or what their input impedance is and generally he couldn't care less. Thus, the concepts of unit loads and fanout operate to save the logic designer a lot of needless problems and work. All that must be remembered is that you cannot drive more unit loads with a gate than its fanout rating. You can, of course, drive less. Suppose a gate with a fanout rating of 10 is required by the logic diagram to drive gates or flip flops whose total unit loads add up to 12. What must be done is to add a device called a line driver to increase the fanout. A line driver is simply an amplifier and is shown on a logic diagram with the standard amplifier symbol of a triangle. Like any other device, the line driver has a unit load rating on its input. Figure 16–1 shows how a line driver can be used to increase the fanout of a gate.

The overwhelming advantage of these integrated logic packages is their low cost and small size. Their disadvantages lie in the fact that the average psychologist lacks the mechanical skill to solder well or to work with fragile subminiature devices. Also the basic power supply voltages which

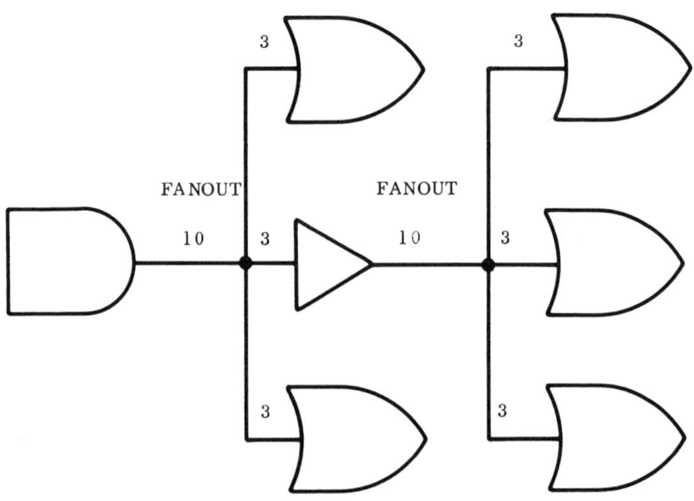

Figure 16–1

do not appear on logic diagrams must be connected to each gate. The devices are quite delicate, and too much twisting of the leads can break them. Lastly, they are also sensitive to heat, and soldering must be done quickly and with a device called a heat sink connected between the joint being soldered and the package. A heat sink is basically a large piece of metal which absorbs heat flowing from the joint being soldered before it reaches the logic package and ruins it.

To get away from these disadvantages, several producers of laboratory equipment have put modules on the market where these basic gates are pre-packaged and connected to patching jacks, and all the user need do is to plug in jumper connections between the basic gates to make the required system connections. The logic symbols for each gate are usually shown connected between the appropriate jacks, and the user need not concern himself with such mundane problems as wiring power to the gates or what the voltage levels corresponding to a 1 or a 0 are. These devices have the additional advantage of being "idiot proof"; i.e., they are impossible to damage by erroneous connections. Design or patching may be done directly in terms of the simpler *and* and *or* logic.

While these systems are very easy to work with, they are extremely expensive. Buying commercially available IC's and building your own patching panels is much cheaper. Since these units are so expensive, it is not usually possible to have as large a variety of gates available as in the do-it-yourself approach. Perhaps the best solution to this dilemma would be for the beginning logic designer to work with these logic kits until he gains enough experience and practice to tackle the more economical μ logic packages directly.

Chapter 17
Switches, Relays, and Relay Logic

A switch is a device which makes or breaks circuit continuity by transforming mechanical movement into contact closures. An ideal switch offers an infinite impedance to the passage of a current when the contacts are open or "broken" and a zero impedance when they are closed or "made."

The contacts in a switch are rated both in terms of the amount of current that they can safely conduct in a steady state and the amount of voltage they can interrupt without arcing or breakdown. Thus a 5 amp, 220 V ac set of switch contacts can safely conduct a current of 5 amps when closed and can interrupt this current from a 220 volt ac source.

The specification of the voltage rating of a switch in terms of ac or dc is very important for the dc voltage rating of a switch is always appreciably less than its ac voltage rating. This is because an ac voltage is "self-quenching." Consider an arc developing across a set of switch contacts breaking an ac current at 60 Hz (cps). When the ac voltage goes to its 0 value, as it will 120 times per second, this arc will be stopped. With dc, however, the voltage level remains constant and once an arc starts it will tend to sustain itself. Arcing causes intense heat, and this heat will evaporate away part of the contact surface thereby pitting it and leaving a poor and erratic contact surface. In some cases contact arcing can permanently weld a set of contacts shut, particularly if the contact is spring actuated as is the case in some types of switches and relays.

Switches are often classified by the number of independent circuits or poles that they can control and also by the number of possible positions available for each pole. Thus a DPDT switch (double pole double throw) can control two independent circuits and has two possible switching positions for each circuit. If a switch has two possible closed positions, the one that is not made when the switch is in the off position is referred to as the NO, or normally open, contact. The one that is made in the off position of the switch is referred to as the NC, or normally closed, contact. The part of the switch that moves from contact to contact while properly called the armature is usually referred to as the arm or common connection of the switch.

A switch wherein the arm can be rotated to contact a large number of output contacts sequentially is called a rotary switch. It also may have one or more poles or independent circuits.

A switch with more than three poles is usually

NC
ARM
NO
SPDT
SPST (NO)
DPDT
DPST (NO)
3
4
5
2
6
1
7
2 POLE; 7 POSITION
ROTARY SWITCH
SPST (NC)
DPST (NC)
(DOTTED LINES INDICATE GANGING OR MECHANICAL COUPLING)
BASIC SWITCH TYPES

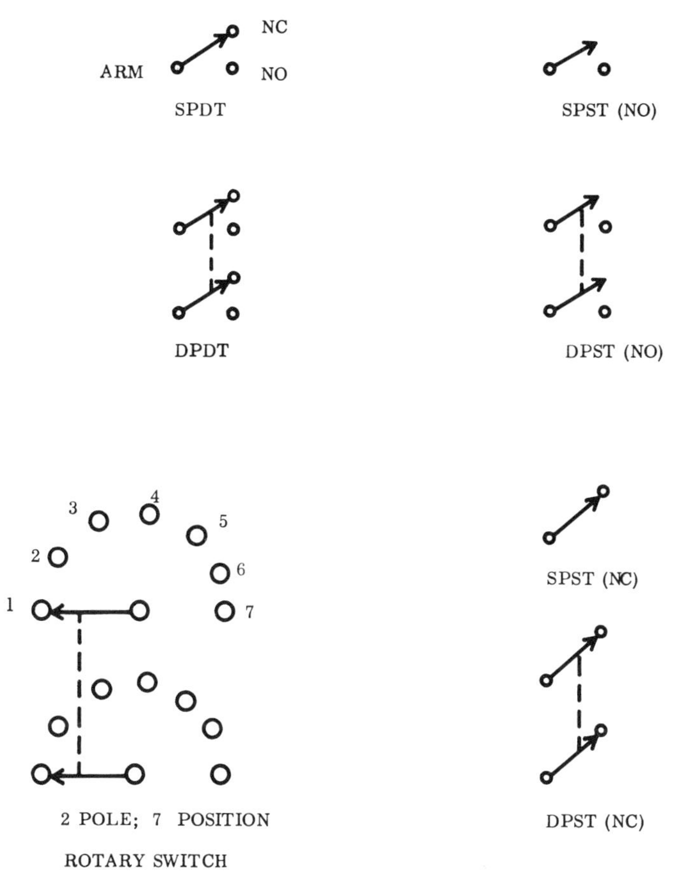

Figure 17–1

referred to as a multipole switch.

Figure 17–1 shows the schematic diagram symbols for a variety of switch configurations and their nomenclature.

In addition to classifying switches by their electrical characteristics, they are also classified independently by their mechanical action. Some of the major types are: toggle switches (actuated by a bat or similarly shaped lever arm), push button switches, rotary switches, slide switches, knife switches, and illuminated switches.

Most switches can be either momentary or permanent. A momentary toggle or push button switch will return to its resting condition when the mechanical pressure actuating it is removed, while a permanent switch will remain in the new position until reset. (Note that a double throw permanent switch is really a mechanically actuated flip flop.)

An illuminated switch consists of an assembly wherein an illuminated message may appear or disappear when the message surface is depressed. These switches may also be momentary or permanent.

A μ switch is not a small switch but a trade name for a device that is actuated by a lever arm which is equipped with a small wheel designed to ride over a cam surface. Hence, it is a cam actuated switch.

The best way to become familiar with the vast array of switching devices available is to write for a few manufacturer's catalogues and study them.

There are two extremely useful standard circuits involving switches, and the reader should become familiar with them.

The first is the interlock circuit. This usually involves nothing more than having a μ switch connected to the cabinet door of a piece of equipment so that when the cabinet door is open, the switch is. This switch contact is then used either directly or indirectly to control the source of power to the equipment. Thus, inexperienced personnel are protected from electrical shock hazard when opening equipment doors. When it is necessary to work on such protected equipment with the power on, the technician must know where this switch is and deliberately actuate it.

The second basic circuit is the double break contact. This is a way of preventing arcing during switch opening (particularly if circuits containing large amounts of inductance have to be opened) by using a double pole instead of a single pole switch and wiring the two poles in series. In this case the full voltage being interrupted does not appear across either contact except momentarily (if one pole opens slightly before the other), and arcing is substantially reduced. Switches designed to interrupt heavy currents usually contain springs to assure rapid action.

DPDT contacts are probably the most useful on a switch. Not all poles or contacts need be used, but they are handy to have available for future modifications to the circuitry. Occasionally a triple pole switch may be available, but because of size limitations for heavy power duty the designer may have to settle for a lesser number of poles or contacts. A DPDT switch is the most common circuit configuration available for toggle switches, whereas a SPDT is the standard for μ switches.

A relay is basically a set of switch contacts that are actuated by an electromagnet as opposed to a mechanical force. Relays are available with all of the contact configurations found in switches and also with multipole DT actions.

The contacts of a relay are rated in the same manner as those of switches. In addition, however, the coil which produces the magnetic field utilized to attract the magnetic armature has its own rating. This rating is usually given in terms of voltage, although some relay coils may be rated in terms of resistance. The voltage rating of a relay is the nominal voltage that its coil is intended to operate at. More specifically, the pull in voltage is that value that will just cause the NO contacts to close, and the drop out voltage is that voltage that will just fail to keep a closed relay closed. In general, it takes a higher voltage to close a relay than to hold it closed.

When a relay coil is de-energized, a spring mechanically opens the contacts and returns them to the NO position.

Relay coils are rated for ac or dc operation. If a dc coil were run on ac, the current would fail to hold the armature closed during the time that the ac voltage approached the drop out value. Hence, the relay would act as a buzzer and chatter audibly.

It can be seen that a relay is an ideal device for the remote control of switching, where the circuit to be controlled is either too inaccessible or too dangerous to be controlled manually. From the point of view of the logic designer, it is a very useful device in that it permits an electric voltage to control a circuit and thus obviates the necessity for manual switching. Hundreds of circuits can be switched simultaneously by the use of relays. Such a feat is manifestly impossible without relays, even if octupi were to be trained as technicians.

A relay is very commonly used as a circuit isolation or an output device. For example, it is usual for the output of a logic system to control the operation of nonlogic devices such as lamps, motors, etc., that operate at totally different voltage levels than those used to indicate a logic 1 or 0. These devices can be controlled by logic circuits by having a logic 1 level signal control a relay coil while the relay contacts apply the larger voltage controlling the ultimate output device.

Many of the basic logic gates already described can be implemented directly by the use of relays, although in a system of any complexity the use of solid state devices or integrated circuits will prove much more economical and practical.

Like switches, relays come in a variety of shapes and sizes. There are DPDT devices about the size of a postage stamp and called postage stamp relays. These come with either solder lugs or with pins that can be plugged into a socket for easy trouble-shooting or replacement. The circuit diagram of this device, showing which pin each of the contacts and the coil are brought out to, is usually stamped right on the case.

Some relays come in hermetically sealed cases for use in extreme environments or in an explosive atmosphere. Hence, these devices are called explosion proof.

Some relays are mounted in transparent cases so that the contact action can be directly observed. These cases can be removed to mechanically actuate the contacts for servicing, or to clean them.

Many relays and switches have what are called self-wiping contacts. This means that in normal operation there is a sliding motion between the closing contacts which tends to keep them polished and eliminates the deleterious effects of pitting.

As with switches, the best way to become acquainted with the plethora of relay types available is to send for a collection of manufacturer's catalogues.

One problem which is often encountered with the use of relays in logic circuits is the problem of racing. This simply means that the actuation times of similar relays is not precisely identical. Hence if a circuit requires simultaneous relay closures, it will probably give a lot of trouble in practice no matter how good the design looks on paper. The designer must, therefore, always be on the lookout for "sneak paths" or circuit configurations that are inadvertently set up in the transient condition after one relay closes but before the other has responded. It should also be realized that the NC contacts will break before the NO contacts close. Some relays and switches are called "shorting" types. In this case, the new contact closure will occur before the old contact breaks.

Within limits, the closure time of a relay can be speeded up by using a somewhat higher coil voltage than the device's rating. Care must be exercised not to use a high enough voltage to burn out the coil. A relay can be slowed in its operation by putting capacity in parallel with its coil.

Since a relay is actuated by energizing a coil which is essentially an inductive device, it follows that when the excitation is removed the magnetic field surrounding the coil tends to collapse rapidly. This in turn generates a counter emf, or voltage, in this coil. Since this voltage is of a magnitude equal to L times the time rate of change of current, and this is quite high, this induced voltage may be many times higher than the coil voltage applied and can do much damage to switch contacts and other parts of the circuit. To prevent this, a diode called a suppression diode may be wired in parallel with the coil in a dc relay, in such a direction that it opposes a current of the polarity used to energize the coil, but permits a current in the inverse direction caused by the collapsing magnetic field to be freely conducted. This prevents the counter emf from being built up to a value that would damage circuit components. In many relays, such as the postage stamp variety, this diode is built in. With such a relay, the coil must be energized with the correct polarity dc, whereas the ordinary dc relay coil can be energized with any polarity. An ac relay coil cannot utilize suppressor diodes, but it will be remembered that ac voltage has self-quenching properties.

Relays have many unique and valuable properties, but when used to implement basic logic gates they suffer from some very serious disadvantages. Among these are the following:

1. They are much more expensive than integrated circuits.
2. They are slow in their action.
3. They are bulky.
4. They are noisy.
5. They have racing problems and problems with contact bounce; i.e., the closure of a relay contact may involve a series of on and off states as the contacts bounce until the device finally settles in the closed condition.
6. They are passive devices and thus require periodic pulse reshaping.

Their one overwhelming advantage for the tyro, however, is that the actual circuitry is simple and easy to understand. If the circuit to be designed is simple and doesn't require more than a few relays, many of the disadvantages are not important. Also a knowledge of basic relay devices can make it possible for the experimenter to design a piece of equipment quickly with whatever components are at hand.

A device which is somewhat in between a relay and a switch is called a stepping switch. This is basically a rotary switch which is driven by the action of a pulse driven solenoid. A stepping pulse momentarily energizes the solenoid which pulls in its armature, which in turn pulls a pawl across a ratchet gear. On the cessation of the pulse, a spring returns the pawl and permits it to rotate the ratchet, thereby advancing the rotary switch one position. Thus, with each incoming stepping pulse, the switch advances one position. After the last position is reached, the next stepping pulse resets the device to the original starting position. As will be seen in the next chapter, stepping switches are ideally suited for use as programing devices.

At this point the reader is ready to follow some of the basic circuits that are commonly used with relays. The plan will be to show some of the things that can be done with a standard DPDT 6 V dc relay to give the reader some feeling for the potential of the device, as well as to illustrate some very useful circuits.

Figure 17–2 illustrates the basic schematic representation of a DPDT relay and shows it hooked up in such a configuration that its coil is energized through one of its own NC contacts when switch S_1 is closed. If this is done, then as soon as the coil of relay K_1 becomes energized it will start to open its NC contacts and remove the source of its own excitation.

Hence, the NC contact will again close, and this entire sequence of events will continue to recur. What will happen is that the relay will act as a buzzer and will continue to vibrate back and forth. This is exactly how a buzzer is built. Unlike a buzzer, there is an additional pole available which is now constantly opening and closing. In effect, a device called a free running multivibrator has been designed. Using a relay as a vibrator is an expensive way to build a doorbell, but the reader will remember that a collapsing magnetic field in a coil is capable of generating a high voltage. Thus, the device of Figure 17–2 can be used as a shocking device by taking the output from the coil. In some cases it may be necessary to run this output through a trans-

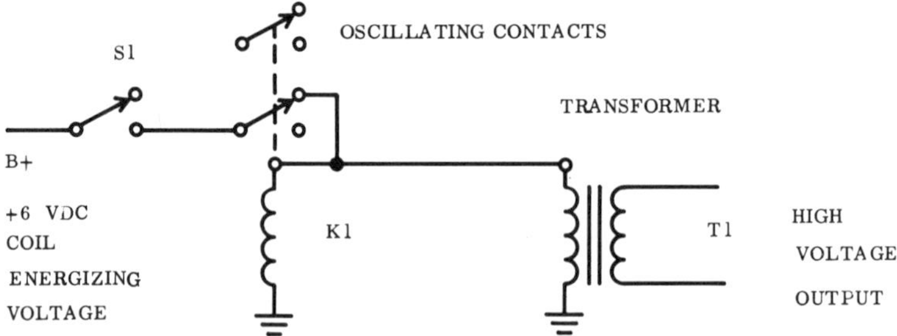

BASIC BUZZER OR SHOCKING DEVICE

Figure 17–2

former to get the desired value of shocking voltage. This device is more illustrative than practical, since unless the relay were mounted remotely the noise that it will make would be a problem for the experimenter.

In many applications it is desirable for a relay to be used as a memory element very similar to a flip flop. Thus if a relay is momentarily excited by a transient pulse, it may be desirable to have the coil stay permanently energized until it is reset. Figure 17–3 shows how this can be accomplished by connecting the arm of one set of contacts to a steady

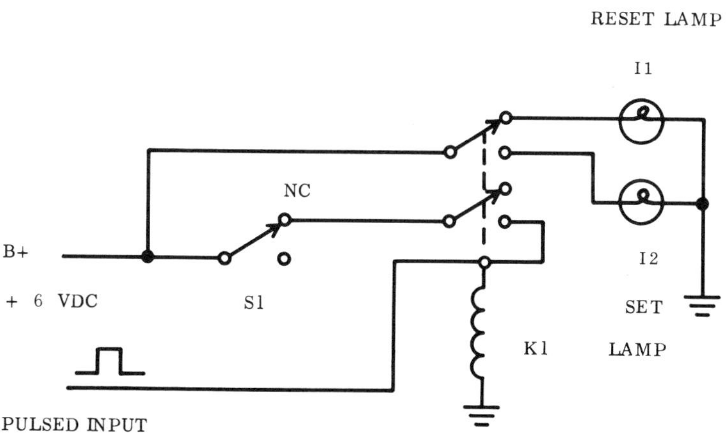

RELAY LOCKING CIRCUIT

Figure 17–3

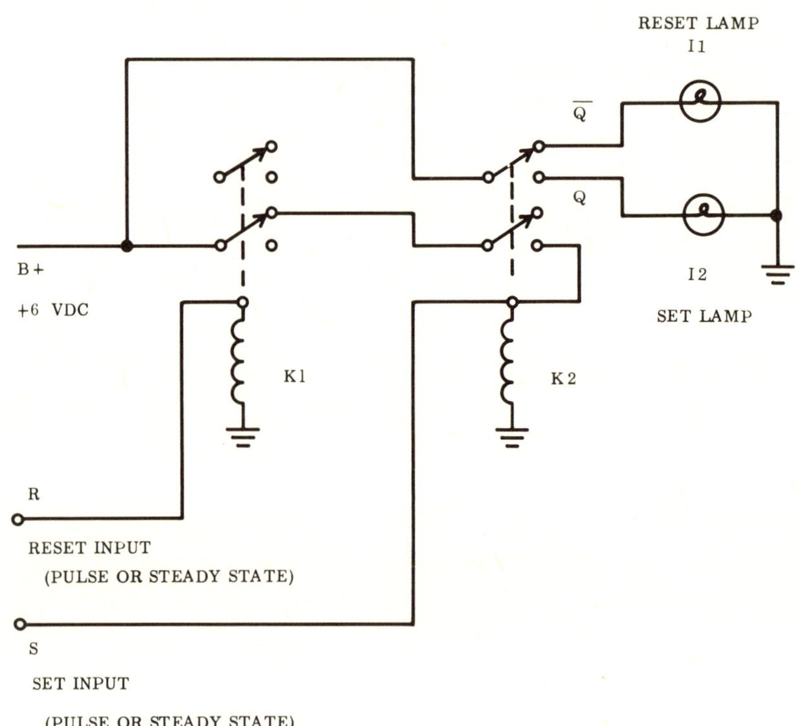

RELAY RS FLIP FLOP

Figure 17–4

voltage (or B+ source as its called) and connecting the NO contact of this set to the coil.

Thus when a transient pulse closes the relay, the locking contacts hold it closed even after the pulse is gone until the reset switch S_1 is actuated to release it. This reset operation can be performed either manually with a switch as illustrated or with another relay. The circuit of Figure 17–3 has had two lights added to indicate the state of the relay. The second pair of contacts has been used to control these lights, and the final circuit is a "pulse catcher," i.e., a device that will indicate if a pulse was ever present on the input line since the device was last cleared or reset. Figure 17–4 shows how the reset switch may be replaced with a second relay, and in effect what has been designed is now an RS flip flop using relays.

Figure 17–5 shows the somewhat trivial design of an *and* and an *or* gate made from relays. It will be noted that, since relays are passive devices, it is not possible to make active gates like nand or nor gates from them.

It is left as an exercise for the reader who enjoys crossword puzzles to design a type T or RST flip flop using relays.

In the following chapter, some of the uses of relays as programing devices will be considered. This area uses some of their unique advantages, and relays cannot usually be replaced by integrated circuits with advantage in such applications.

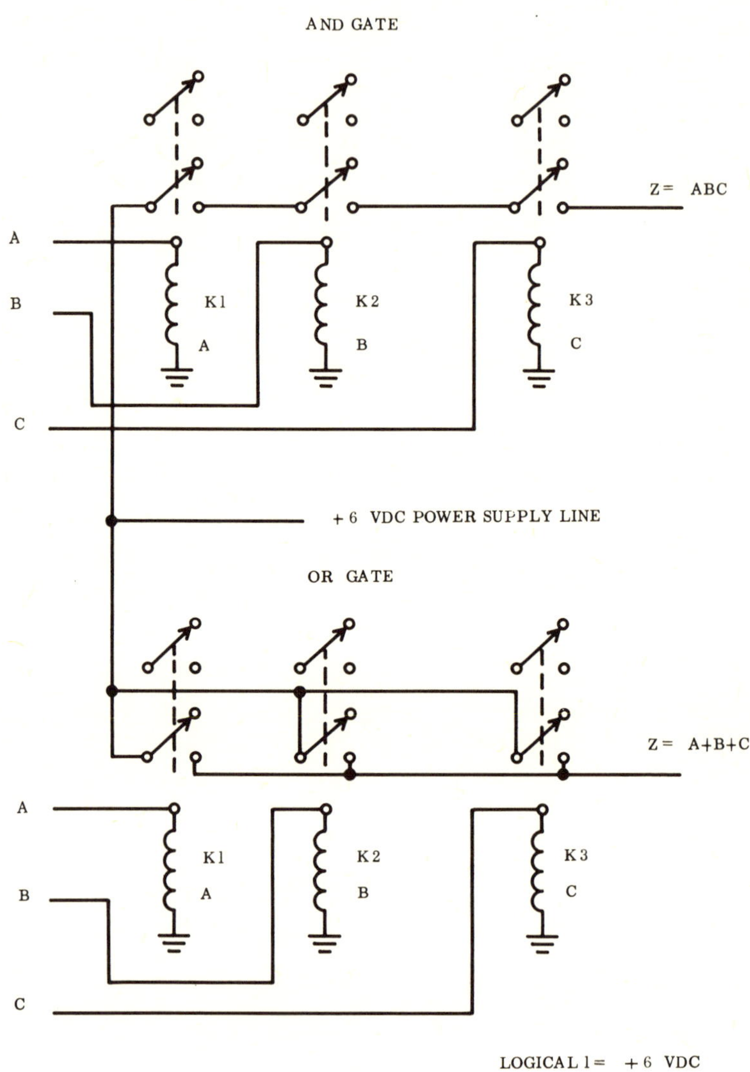

RELAY <u>AND</u> AND <u>OR</u> GATES

Figure 17–5

Chapter 18
Programing Devices

A program is a predetermined sequence of operations that is performed by a system. A program may be entirely preplanned *ab initio,* or it may have contingent elements or branching. (Branching is a programing technique where there are several possible subsequent operations and the results at a junction point in the program determine which of the alternative possibilities is selected.) A system may be hard wired to perform only one program as in the case of a special purpose device, or it may be programable, permitting a variety of different programs to be performed at different times.

While large commercial computers may be programed by means of magnetic tape or punched cards, the type of programing used in a piece of experimental equipment is most likely to involve the use of one of the three basic methods to be described in this chapter. These are stepping switches, relay trees, and punched tape readers.

STEPPING SWITCH PROGRAMING

Figure 18–1 shows how a stepping switch can be used to control a group of output devices sequentially. For the sake of concreteness, the output devices shown here are lamps which are used to illuminate stimulus words, but they could just as well be relays used to control any electrically operated device like a motor, a shocker, etc. In the case of this illustrative design, each lamp will represent a bit in a binary number, and the device of Figure 18–1 has been designed as a decimal counter that will count incoming stepping pulses from 0 to 9 and then reset to 0.

It can be observed from Figure 18–1 that the output lines from each position of the stepping switch can be connected to any combination of lights or other output devices that it is desired to activate in that step of the program. In the example used, lines 0 through 9 are used to illuminate that combination of lights that add up to the binary number of the switch position. It will also be noticed that each output device or lamp is connected to the switch contact through a diode. This diode is connected in such a direction that it permits the positive energizing voltage to pass a current to the desired lights, but it prevents the passage of current to other lines connected to the lamp thereby isolating them. If isolation diodes were not used, the stepping switch would need a separate pole for each of the lights to assure isolation. In this case a four

CR 2
CR 3
CR 4
CR 5
CR6
CR 7
CR 8
CR 9
CR 10
CR 11
CR 12
CR 13
CR 14
CR 15
CR 16
CR 1
I1 (1)
I2 (2)
I3 (4)
I4 (8)
STEP
PULSE
S1
B +
+6 VDC
PULSE GENERATOR
PULSE OUT
K1
K2
STEPPING SWITCH PROGRAMER

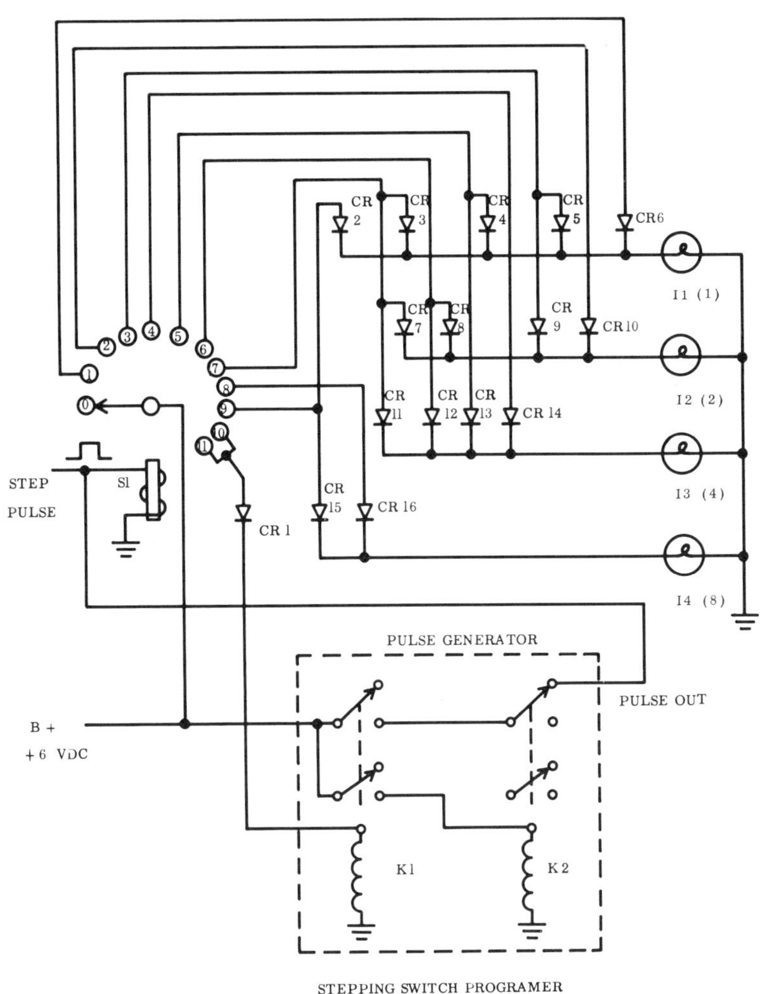

Figure 18-1

pole stepping switch, instead of the one pole switch used, would be necessary.

Since only ten positions of the stepping switch are needed for a decimal counter, all positions beyond ten are simply connected together and used to step the switch to the last position. Since the stepping switch requires a pulse to step, relays K_1 and K_2 are used to form a pulse generator to step the switch completely around before the next regular stepping pulse arrives to reset the switch to 0. If a ten position stepping switch was available, this pulse generator would be unnecessary.

The way the pulse generator works is as follows. When the stepping switch reaches position 10, K_1's coil is energized. This closes the NO contacts of K_1 and starts a pulse through the NC contact of K_2. However at the same time, the other NO contact of K_1 energizes the coil of K_2 and thus terminates the pulse. When the stepping switch is between positions 10 and 11, K_1 is deenergized which in turn unlocks K_2 and sets the pulse generator up for its next operation. This circuit cannot be used if the stepping switch has shorting contacts since in such a case both relay coils would remain locked.

Stepping switches are commonly available up to about 25 positions, which means that they can readily be used to implement 25-step programs. Figure 18–2 shows how two or more stepping switches can be cascaded to increase the number of programing steps obtainable.

If as in Figure 18–2 two independent 10-posi-

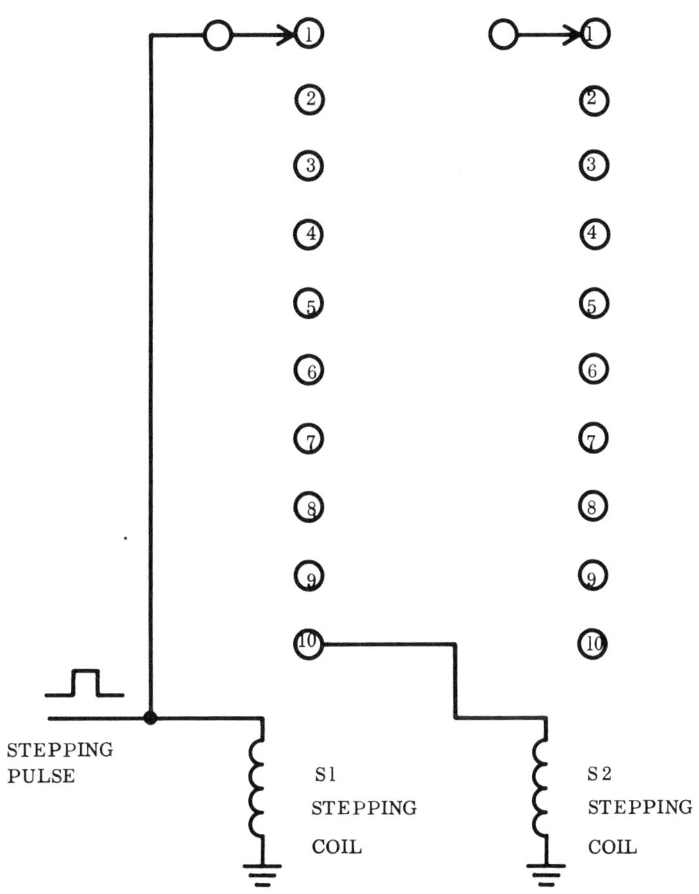

CASCADED CONTROL DECKS OF TWO STEPPING SWITCHES

Figure 18–2

tion stepping switches are connected so that one switch can only step when the other switch is in the last position, then there are 10×10 or 100 different combinations of switches 1 and 2. One pole of one of these switches has been tied up for this cascading, but the remainder can be used to control lines that operate the devices being controlled.

With a little thought the reader will realize that to provide 100 different program lines from two 10-position stepping switches with their control poles or decks cascaded requires that one of the switches have 10 poles as shown in Figure 18–3.

Another way of accomplishing the same result without the need of such an expensive and bulky stepping switch would be by combining two stepping switches with one and two poles respectively with a set of 20 relays. One pole of one stepping switch is used to control the stepping as shown in Figure 18–2 while the remaining two independent poles are used to actuate the relays as shown in Figure 18–4.

It will be noticed that the relays from 1 to 10 require only SPST (NO) contact, but relays 11 through 20 require 10 NO poles. Such multipole relays are available, but they can also be made up of a collection of DPDT relays by connecting their coils in parallel.

Relay Trees

A relay tree is basically a device wherein the contacts of a set of relays are cascaded to form the

PROGRAM LINE 5 OF TWO CASCADED STEPPING SWITCHES

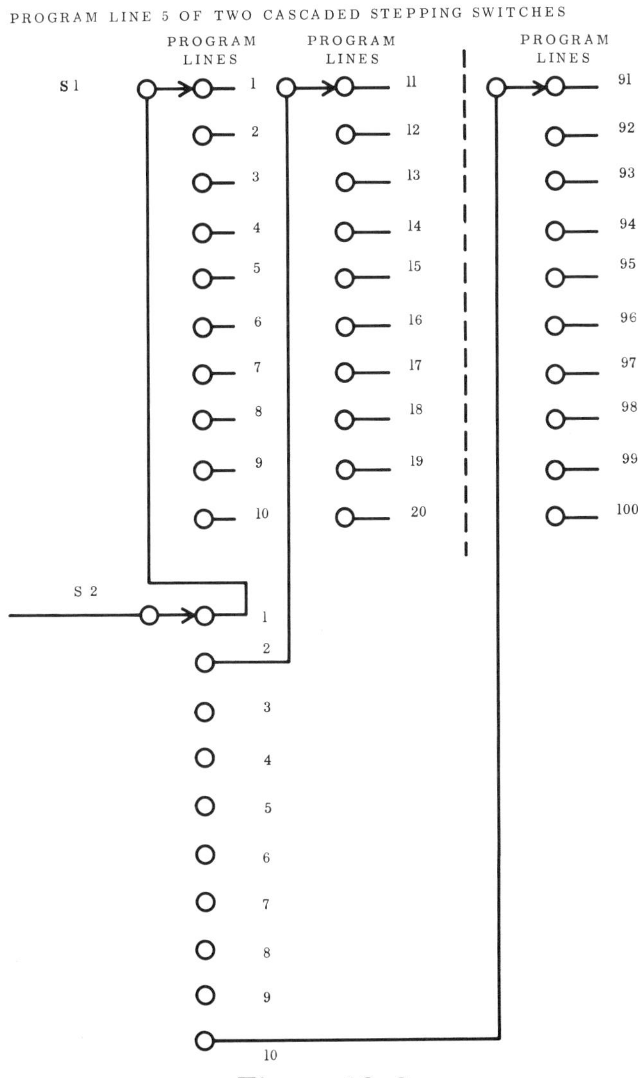

Figure 18–3

S2   S1
K1   K11
K2   K12
K3   K13
K4   K14
K5   K15
K6   K16
K7   K17
K8   K18
K9   K19
K10   K20

K1
K11 A
B +
PROGRAM LINE 1
K12 A
PROGRAM LINE 2
(TO RELAYS K13 A – K20 A)
K2
K11 B
PROGRAM LINE 11
(TO RELAYS K12 B – K20 B)
K10
K11 J
PROGRAM LINE 91
(TO RELAYS K12 J – K20 J)

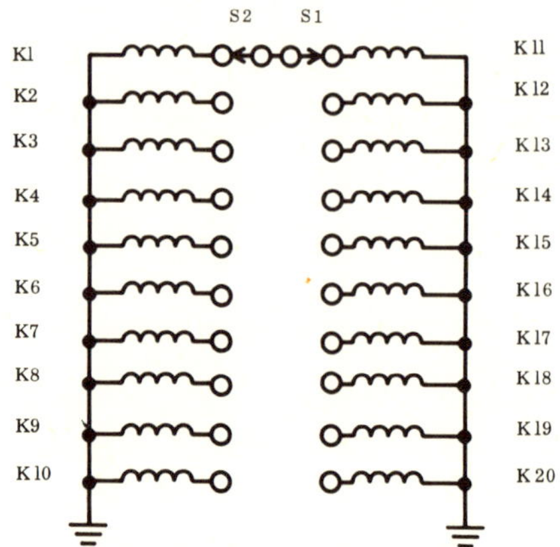

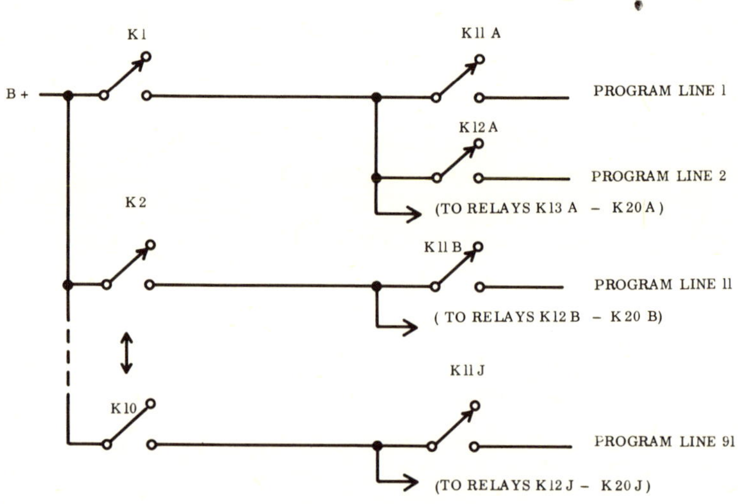

Figure 18-4

equivalent of an electrically actuated rotary switch. Figure 18–5 shows a relay tree made up of basic DPDT relays with eight output lines each of which can be used to control a step in a program or actuate some device.

The operation of the relay tree, shown in the schematic of Figure 18–5, can best be followed in terms of the following truth table which shows the required condition of each relay (or parallel combination of relays) to produce an output on each of the eight output lines. A 1 indicates that the relay is energized, and a 0 indicates that it is de-energized.

		Output Line							
		0	1	2	3	4	5	6	7
Coil circuit	A	0	1	0	1	0	1	0	1
	B	0	0	1	1	0	0	1	1
	C	0	0	0	0	1	1	1	1

The reader should verify the truth table by tracing the pathways through the relay contacts on each of the eight permutations of control inputs A, B, and C. In effect what has been done is to design a rotary switch that is electrically rather than mechanically actuated.

It should be obvious from Figure 18–5 that for a four output relay tree only two stages would be needed while for a two output tree only one relay with a SPDT contact would be needed. Similarly 16 outputs could be obtained with four stages. The final stage would of course require eight poles which

A
SCHEMATIC DIAGRAM
OUTPUT LINES
1
2
3
4
K3A
5
6
7
8
INPUT
(ARM)
C
K1
B
K2
A
K3B
B
FUNCTIONAL DIAGRAM
1
2
3
4
5
6
7
8
INPUT
OUTPUT LINES
C
B
A
CONTROL LINES
RELAY TREE

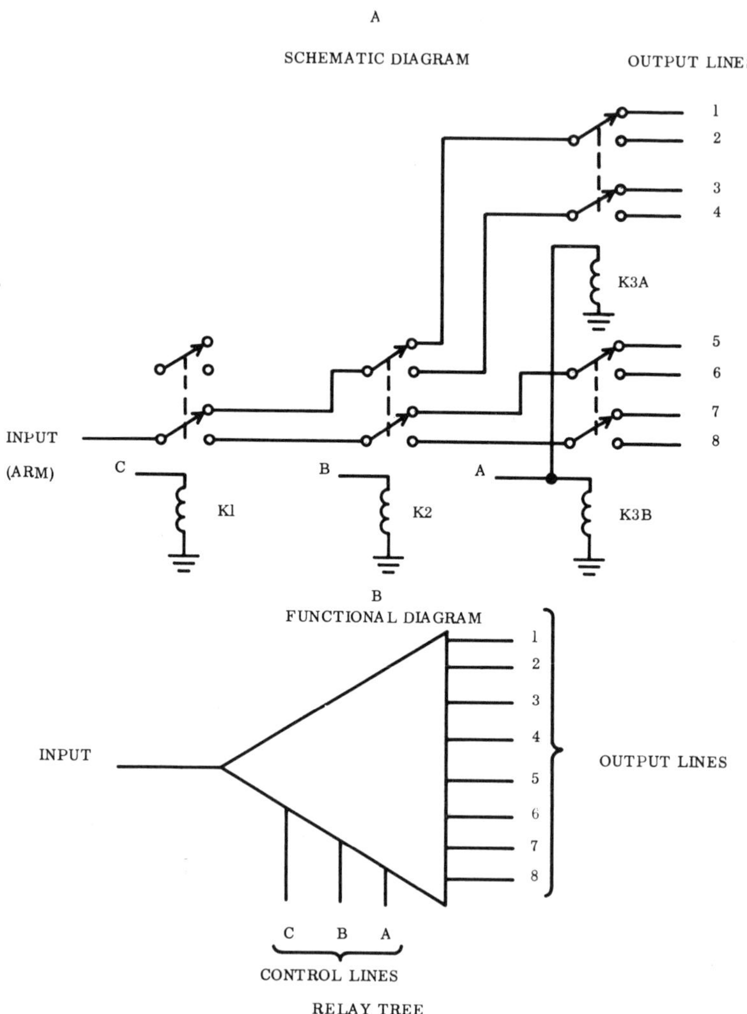

Figure 18–5

could be obtained by paralleling the coils of four DPDT relays. In this case the truth table would have to be expanded to account for four control input lines.

Thus, it is apparent that the number of output lines increases in powers of 2 so that the number of output lines controlled by a relay tree is 2^N, where $N =$ the number of independent relays or stages.

It follows from the foregoing that a relay tree is ideally suited for selecting stimuli automatically. It does everything that a rotary switch can do without the need of manual or mechanical actuation. The only remaining question is how can this switch be "rotated" automatically. A study of the truth table shown provides the answer. If input lines $A, B,$ and C are properly weighted as 1, 2, and 4, respectively, then the numbers shown in the truth table represent the binary numbers from 0 to 7. Hence the stepping of this "switch" can be accomplished by feeding the appropriate output bits of a modulus 8 counter to the three control lines as shown in Figure 18–6.

The actual time of stepping will of course be controlled by the incoming stepping pulse to the counter as in the case of a stepping switch. Also, as in the case of a stepping switch, this stepping pulse can be from a time base, causing each stimulus to be presented for a fixed time, or made contingent on some response on the part of a subject.

Basically both stepping switch and relay tree programing are primarily suited for permanent programs that are hardwired into the equipment.

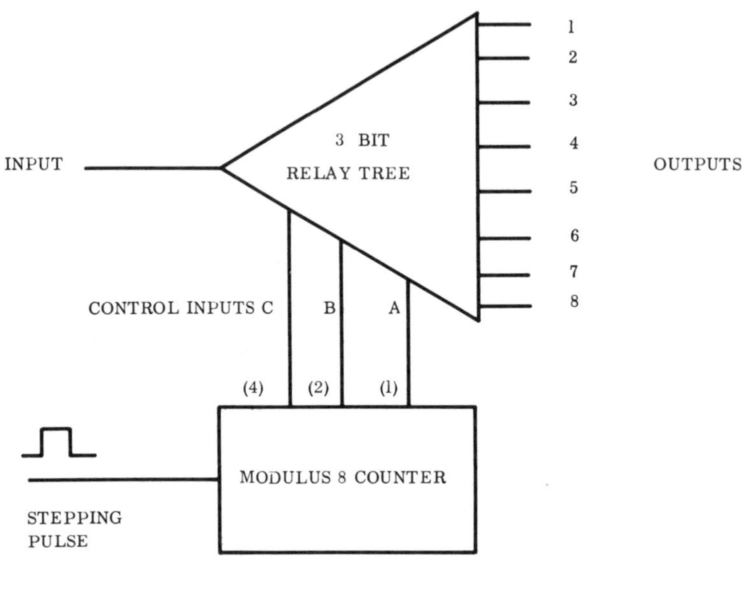

COUNTER CONTROLED RELAY TREE

Figure 18–6

They may however be made reprogramable, and thus more flexible, by the use of what are called patch panels. A patch panel is simply a collection of jacks into which external cables may be plugged. By bringing out all switch and relay contacts to these patching points, it is possible to temporarily hook up all possible configurations of the equipment and tear them down or modify them when desired. This is certainly the approach that should be taken by anyone concerned with experimental equipment design or prototype work. There are one of two possible approaches that can be taken with patch panels of any degree of complexity. The first is to lay out all patching jacks in columns and rows, designated by numbers and letters respectively, and list the function of each jack in a table. Thus, jack 21-K may be found to represent the NO contact of contact set *A* of relay K-15. The other approach is to lay out a schematic of the device right on the face of the patch panel so that the function of the jacks can be seen at a glance. The latter method results in a patch panel that is harder to build and more wasteful of space but much easier to work with.

There are also available some very expensive patch panels that function like connectors. Many programs may be patched on different panels and left permanently set up to be plugged into a female connector that is actually connected to the circuitry involved. Connecting these devices requires the use of tables, but once programed and tested they can be switched into operation in a matter of seconds.

A device which is specifically designed to permit the rapid changing of programs or the rapid transfer from one to another is the punched tape reader.

PUNCHED TAPE READERS

A tape reader is a device that responds to holes punched in a paper or synthetic tape that is advanced in discrete steps by a stepping pulse. There are two basic types with respect to the method employed to read the tape. One type uses spring actuated plungers that ride over each column of holes and produce electrical continuity when a hole is punched in the tape and the absence of continuity when the hole is uncut. This type suffers from a build up of insulating material on the plunger, from the tape it rides over, and this ultimately results in erratic contacts. To get around this difficulty a more expensive type of tape reader utilizes photo electric cells for each bit or plunger position which indicates the presence of a hole in the tape by responding electrically to the passage of a beam of light through the hole.

Tape readers may also be divided into line and block readers. A line reader responds to only one line on a tape and is usually limited to about eight bits. A block reader on the other hand reads several lines at each step and may have over 160 bits available. Naturally, a block reader reading eight lines of eight bits each will advance eight lines with each stepping pulse.

During the transit time of the tape between program steps, some circuitry is required to prevent the traveling holes from producing transient effects in the system. This is usually done by requiring a read signal at each step before an output from the tape reader is applied to the system. An NO multipole relay with one pole for each bit is a common way of providing this necessary feature. Thus, the read signal which is derived from the stepping mechanism of the tape reader is used to energize the coil of this relay, and the contacts connect the plunger outputs to the circuitry to be controlled.

Each control line from the tape reader can be used in exactly the same way that the output lines of a stepping switch or relay tree were to control stimuli producing or other devices. The same need for isolation diodes and the prevention of unintended "sneak paths" is also present.

Programing is accomplished by cutting holes in the tape either manually or with special machines. This involves tabulating what each bit controls in the system and then deciding what system conditions are wanted in each successive step. In the case of a tape program, however, the number of steps in the program is limited only by the length of the tape. Programs can be changed in a matter of seconds by simply changing tapes.

Perhaps the most interesting problem in programing involves the area of contingent programing or branching. Alternative possibilities for a program can be built in with the type of programing devices discussed herein in one of two ways. The first method involves controlling the number of steps that a programing device advances as a function of the subject's responses. The second method involves switching to different programers as a function of subject response. This latter catagory would also include the use of the subject's responses to set up stimulus conditions for the next step by the use of logical memory devices. Both of these methods basically involve requiring subject responses to set up the conditions for a "go" signal for the next step. Different mutually exclusive combinations of responses can be used to set up go conditions for several possible alternative next steps.

For the sake of illustration, consider that in response to stimulus N in a program the subject may depress one of three switches, S_1, S_2, or S_3.

There are several ways that this switch closure can be translated into different stimulus presentations in step $N + 1$ of the program. If a stepping switch or a relay tree is used as a programing device, each switch may be connected to a different stepping pulse generator that initiates a chain of pulses of differing number thereby stepping the program to different conditions. Each switch could also be used to control a multipole relay which in turn could connect all of the stimulus presenting output devices to a different programer, thus accomplishing the branching.

If program advance is not to be time controlled but instead made contingent on a correct subject response, all that need be done is to use a logic gate that requires a correct switch closure as a condition precedent for program advancement. Different switch closures may be required for different steps in a program. For example, with an eight bit tape reader, bits A and B may be used to set the stepping requirements for a particular step from among four possible response switches in accordance with the following truth table:

	State	0	1	2	3
Control bit	A (1)	0	1	0	1
	B (2)	0	0	1	1
Switch required for step	1	1	0	0	0
	2	0	1	0	0
	3	0	0	1	0
	4	0	0	0	1

From this truth table the reader should have no difficulty in writing the required logic diagram as shown in Figure 18–7.

To complicate the situation a little, suppose that the go condition for a program step is now not the pressing of the correct switch but the pressing of three switches in the required sequence, i.e., S1, then S2, and finally S3. Obviously this requires the use of some sort of memory device. Figure 18–8 shows how this system requirement may be implemented utilizing flip flops and logic gates. Figure 18–9 shows how this same requirement can be readily implemented using relays with locking circuits.

A study of Figure 18–8 and 18–9 should show the reader what logic functions are performed by the relays in Figure 18–9. Thus, the logic diagram of Figure 18–8 is a general solution of the problem, while the schematic diagram of Figure 18–9 is a specific solution.

It is apparent that relays K3 and K4 of Figure 18–9 cannot lock shut until the relay (or relays) preceding them in the sequence is closed, and therefore the sequential operation requirement is ful-

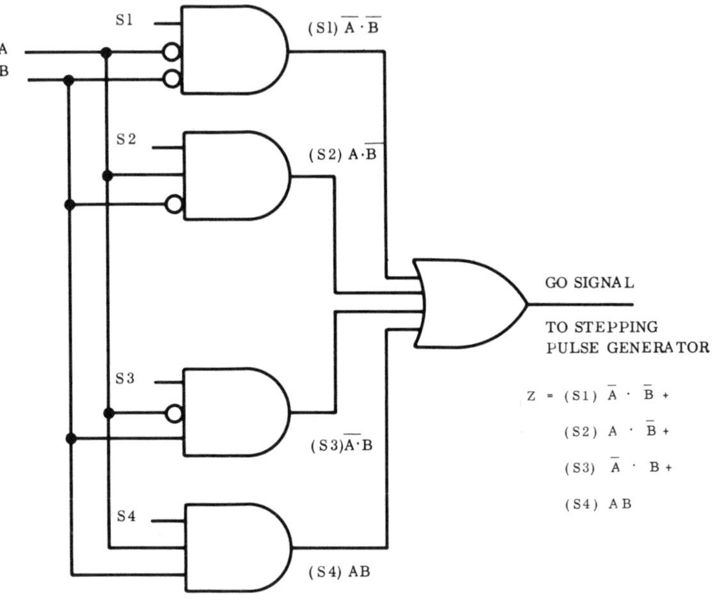

GO OR STEPPING CONDITION AS A FUNCTION OF BITS A AND B

Figure 18–7

S3*
S2*
S1*
*MOMENTARY SWITCH
1 LEVEL
LINE
GO OUTPUT
C
R   Q
FF_B
S   Q
B
R   Q
FF_A
S   Q
CLEAR
OR RESET
LINE

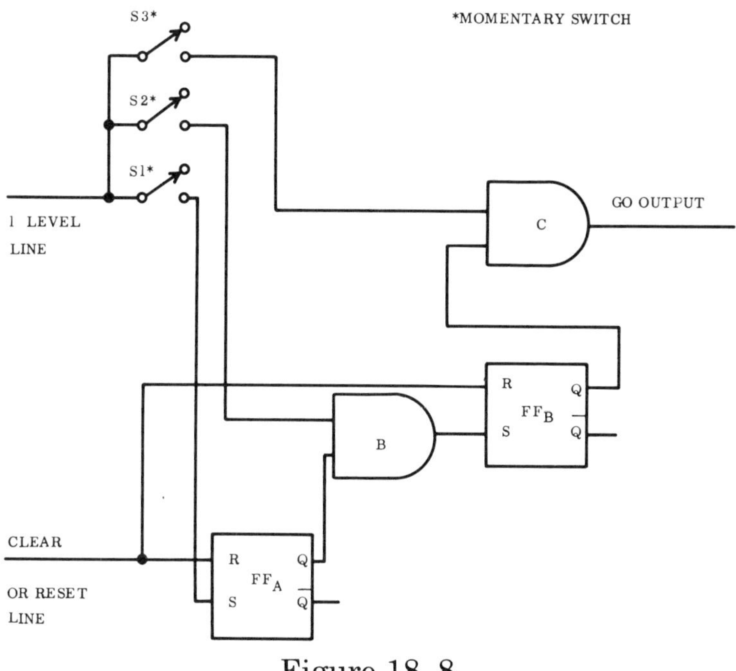

Figure 18–8

STEPPING PULSE
OR GO SIGNAL
GO OUTPUT
B +
RESET OR
CLEAR
PULSE
K1
K2
K3
K4
S1*
S2*
S3*
*MOMENTARY

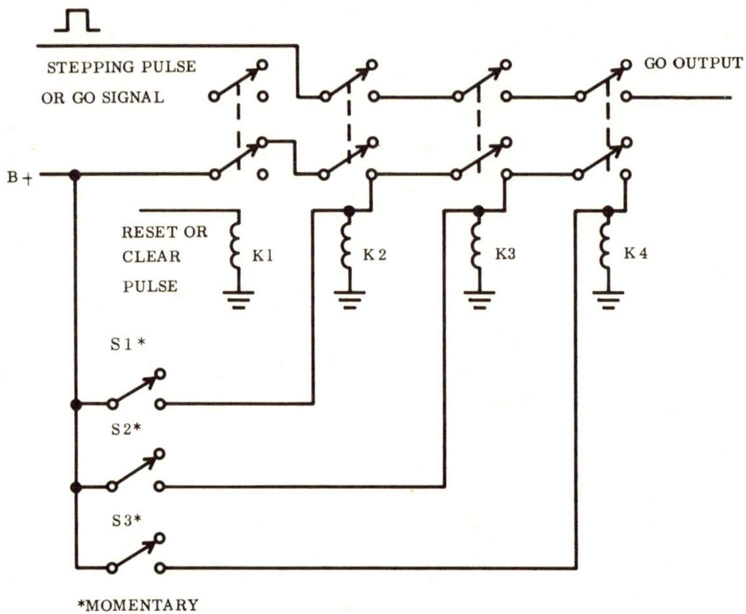

Figure 18–9

filled. However if two switches were actuated simultaneously a locking could result. This is analogous to the racing problem mentioned in chapter 17. This drawback could be eliminated by the addition of time delay devices (or mechanically preventing the simultaneous operation of two or more switches).

It will be noted in the present design that all that is required for a go or program stepping signal is that the three switches be depressed in the correct order. If it were desired to make the go requirement that all switches be depressed in the correct order and that no incorrect responses be made in between, then some device would have to be added to clear all relays or flip flops every time an erroneous or out of sequence response was made. In effect such a device would require one perfect trial as a condition precedent to advance the program. It is left as an exercise for the reader to modify the diagrams of Figures 18–8 and 18–9 to incorporate such a feature.

Chapter 19
Nonlogic or Analogue Devices

If the reader has mastered all of the material presented to this point, he now knows all he will ever have to know about logic design and its methods. If he will obtain an assortment of inexpensive commercial logic packages and experiment with them for a while in his own lab, he will very rapidly acquire a familiarity with their use. In a surprisingly short time, he will be able to design many simple devices intuitively and will only have to resort to some of the more formal design methods presented herein for solving the more complicated problems. He will also probably be able to improve upon and simplify the designs of others including those of commercial equipment designers. Very often with a little modification a commercial device can be made to do a lot of useful things that its designer never intended.

What remains to be mastered is a collection of extremely useful devices that are essentially nonbinary or nonlogic in their operation but are very often used in actual systems in connection with the logic circuitry. These devices, which may have an infinite variety of signal levels, are referred to as analogue as opposed to digital devices.

OPERATIONAL AMPLIFIERS

Many useful analogue devices are based on the operation of a basic component called an operational amplifier. An operational amplifier is a special type of amplifier. Like any amplifier, it provides a gain or an increase in amplitude of the output over the input, but the two special features that set it apart from all other amplifiers are that it has:

1. An open loop gain of infinity.
2. An infinite input impedance.

The term "open loop gain" refers to the gain of an amplifier in the absence of feedback. Feedback refers to the feeding of some portion of the output signal back to the input signal. If the feedback signal is in phase with the input and acts to increase the stage gain, it is called positive feedback. If the feedback signal is out of phase with the input and tends therefore to lower the stage gain, it is called negative feedback. Operational amplifiers are always used in a circuit with negative feedback for if an amplifier had an infinite gain any input signal no matter how small would cause an infinite output. Since no device can supply an infinite current what would happen with an open loop operational amplifier is that it would saturate at the maximum output level that it was capable of and would in fact be a binary device having only two states, 0 output or saturated output. Since most operational amplifiers are dc amplifiers, it follows that they can be saturated either in a positive or negative direction and can be toggled back and forth by the appropriate input signal polarity. As a practical matter no amplifier can be built to have an infinite open loop gain, but to qualify as an operational amplifier a device should have a very high open loop gain. Practical amplifiers can provide open loop gains, or ratios of output to input levels, in excess of 100,000.

The fact that an operational amplifier theoretically has an infinite input impedance means that it doesn't load or draw a current from the input circuit driving it. Practical input impedances of several megohms are attainable.

Figure 19–1 shows a practical configuration or circuit for the use of an operational amplifier. Resistors R_1 and R_2 provide the feedback needed, and their ratio determines the actual closed loop gain of the device. The explanation of why the closed loop gain, A, equals R_2/R_1 requires slightly more electronic sophistication than the reader can reasonably be expected to have at this point, but if he will accept the author's assurance that this is in fact the case, he will be able to understand and utilize all of the applications of operational amplifiers.

The simple formula $A = R_2/R_1$ says that an operational amplifier (op amp) is a device whose gain is determined only by the ratio of two resistors. Thus,

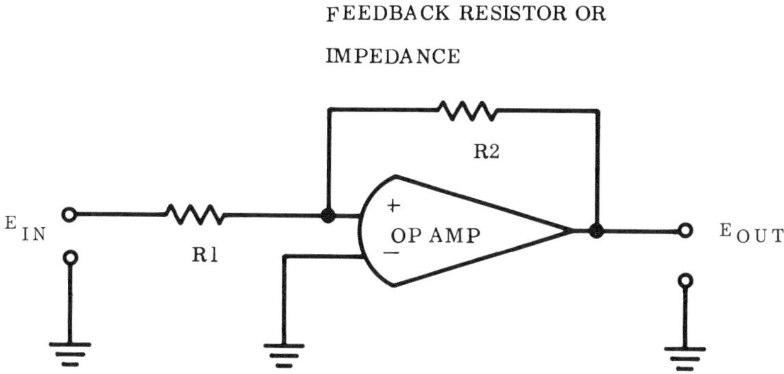

Figure 19–1

an operational amplifier can be set to any gain desired (up to its open loop value) by simply selecting the appropriate resistors. More importantly, since the closed loop gain depends only on this ratio of two resistors and nothing else, it follows that the gain can be set as accurately as desired by simply using resistors of the required accuracy.

As a practical matter, the closed loop gain of an op amp is limited not only by the open loop gain capabilities of the amplifier but also by the input signal and noise levels that it is to be used with, since a relatively small noise level can put a sensitive amplifier into the saturated state very rapidly.

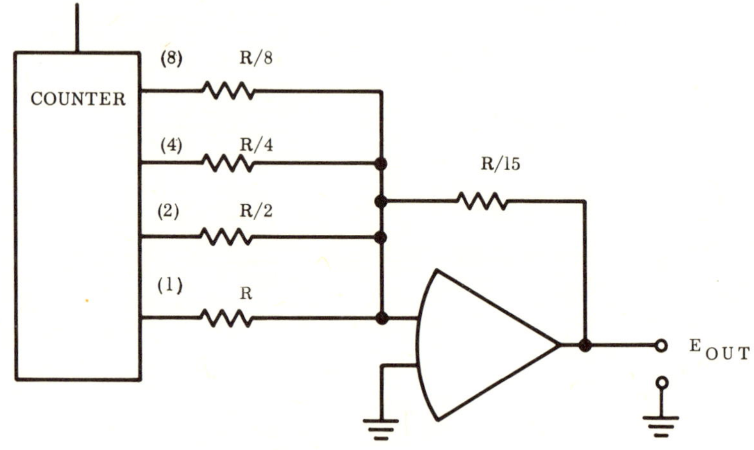

DIGITAL TO ANALOGUE (D TO A) CONVERTER

Figure 19-2

The basic characteristics of an op amp have been described. What remains to be done is to show some of the ways in which these properties can be practically utilized.

D to A Converters

Figure 19-2 shows how an operational amplifier can be used to convert a digital signal to an equivalent analogue or proportional voltage. In this common D to A converter each bit of the binary number

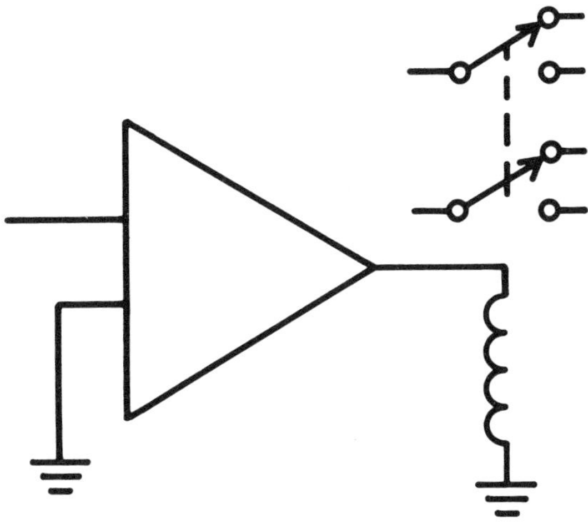

Figure 19–3

is differentially weighted by the ratio of the feedback resistor to its input resistor.

Thus, each bit is weighted as a 1, 2, 4, or 8, and the voltage output of the amplifier is the sum of the 1 level bits.

Relay Drivers

Figure 19–3 shows a schematic representation of an amplifier used to drive a relay coil. This device makes it possible for a 1 level logic signal to actuate a relay whose coil requires a different voltage level and more power than is present as a logic 1 signal. In effect it permits the converting of a logic 1 (or 0 signal) into a switch closure (or opening), thereby enabling the control of a wide range of output devices (e.g., lamps, motors, buzzers, etc.) by the logic system.

Difference Amplifiers

A difference amplifier is a device whose output level is a function of the difference in amplitude of two input signals.

If a dc operational amplifier is used and if its output is fed through a diode to drive a relay coil, the level detector of Figure 19–4 results. This level detector will energize the relay when the signal input is some small value (e.g., 1 MV) more positive than the reference voltage (or more negative depending on how the internal diode is connected). Thus, a signal indicating that a voltage has exceeded some level preset on the reference input will be given by a relay closure. When below this threshold, the relay will remain open.

Figure 19–5 shows how two of these amplifiers can be used to detect whether the voltage monitored is within, above or below preset limits. If the amplitude of the voltage being monitored is the analogue of some response on the part of the experimental subject, the three possible permutations of relay closures can form the basis of a program branching or decision making functions.

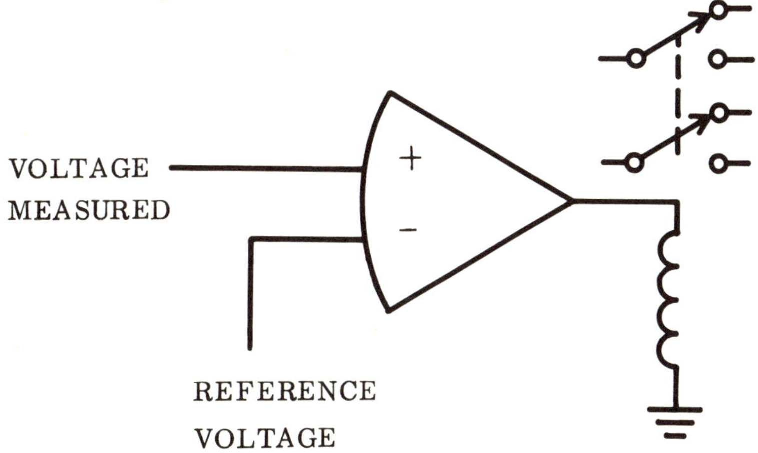

Figure 19–4

Also, the circuit of Figure 19–5 is useful in its own right to monitor that an input variable is held between preset limits.

TIMERS

Timers may involve the use of multivibrators and counters as previously mentioned, or they may involve the use of an electric motor clock. These latter units are nondigital devices and usually contain terminals to start, stop, and reset the motor

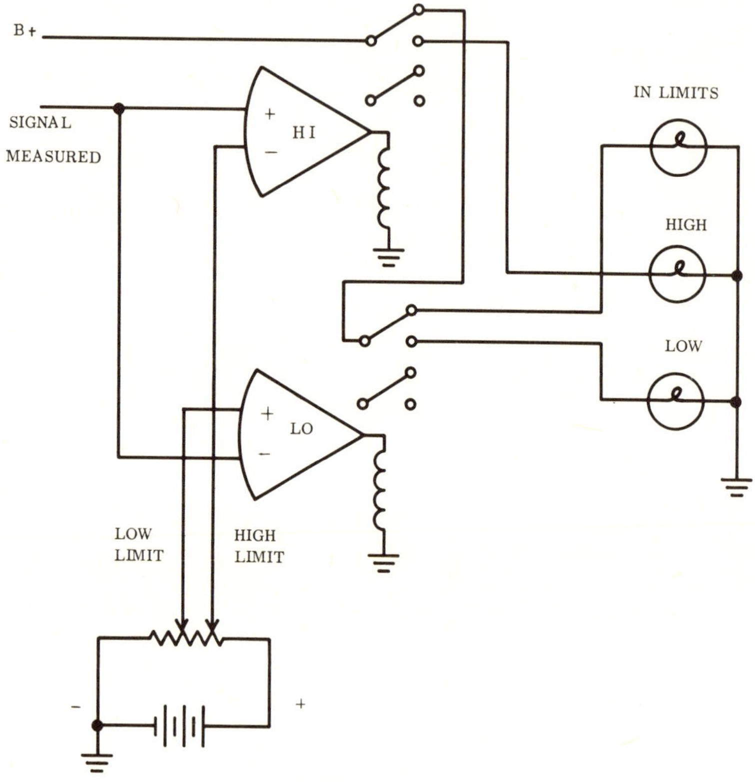

UPPER AND LOWER LIMIT DETECTOR

Figure 19–5

with a control signal. Output switches are usually provided that actuate on the starting of the motor, and on the completion of the timed period providing a useful output.

If many different timing periods are needed, a syncronous electric motor may be used to drive an axle containing a group of cams. Each cam will then control the opening and closing of a particular μ switch as shown in Figure 19–6.

NUMERIC AND ALPHA-NUMERIC READOUTS

Very often the output of a logical system will be a numerical indication or a group of letters, symbols, or words. If there are only a few potential outputs, these may be written on the faces of a set of legend lights, and the logic system may be used to illuminate the appropriate lamps. Ordinary indicator lamps can be located next to a set of legend cards to accomplish the same purpose more economically, with the drawback that now all of the messages are always readable and hence the emphasis on the selected message or stimulus is lacking.

In cases where there are too large a number of potential message readouts for these approaches to be practical, numeric or alpha-numeric readouts may be used.

A common type of numeric display contains a sandwich of transparent Plexiglass plates stacked one behind the other. Each plate has a different number or symbol engraved on it. It is possible by

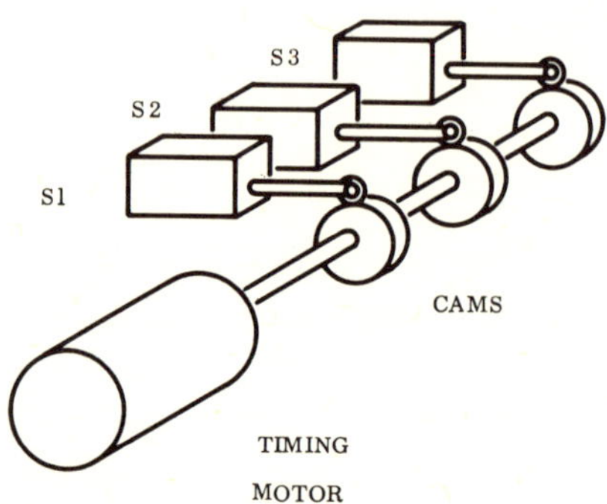

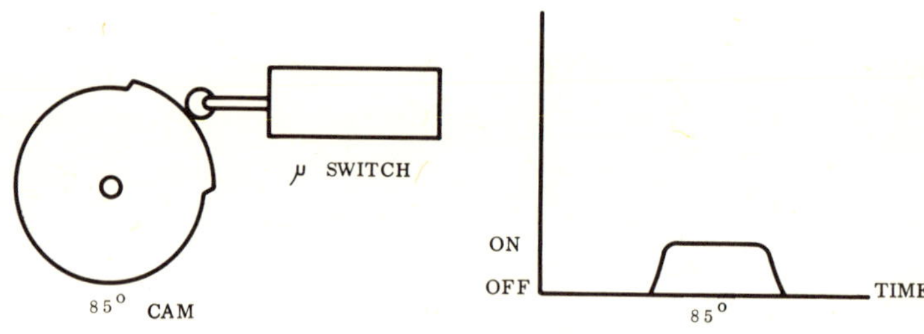

CAM TIMER

Figure 19–6

energizing the correct input pin to edge-light any one of these plates individually. When this is done the engraved numeral will light up and the device will display the appropriate number or symbol.

Since the elements of the display are stacked in line and since they require a minimum thickness to be engraved, it is not practical to have more than about 12 plates in a tube. More than 12 plates results in a barrel vision effect which requires that the viewer be directly in front of the readout.

Commercially available numeric tubes therefore usually contain 12 symbols (the numerals from 0–9 and a + and − sign). A display made up of three numeric tubes is thus capable of reading out any number from 0–999 or from 0–99 if a sign is to be included.

To get around these limitations alpha-numeric tubes were developed. These also may consist of a stack of etched transparent Plexiglass plates, but instead of characters being etched on the plates each plate contains a single straight line with a different position and orientation as illustrated in Figure 19–7. By simultaneously illuminating one or more of these lines, all of the letters of the alphabet and all of the numerals, plus some additional special symbols, may be formed.

Alpha-numeric tubes in general do not have as good a form factor as numeric tubes due to the way that the displayed characters must be formed. Also if a single lamp is out, an erroneous character rather than a dark tube face may be displayed.

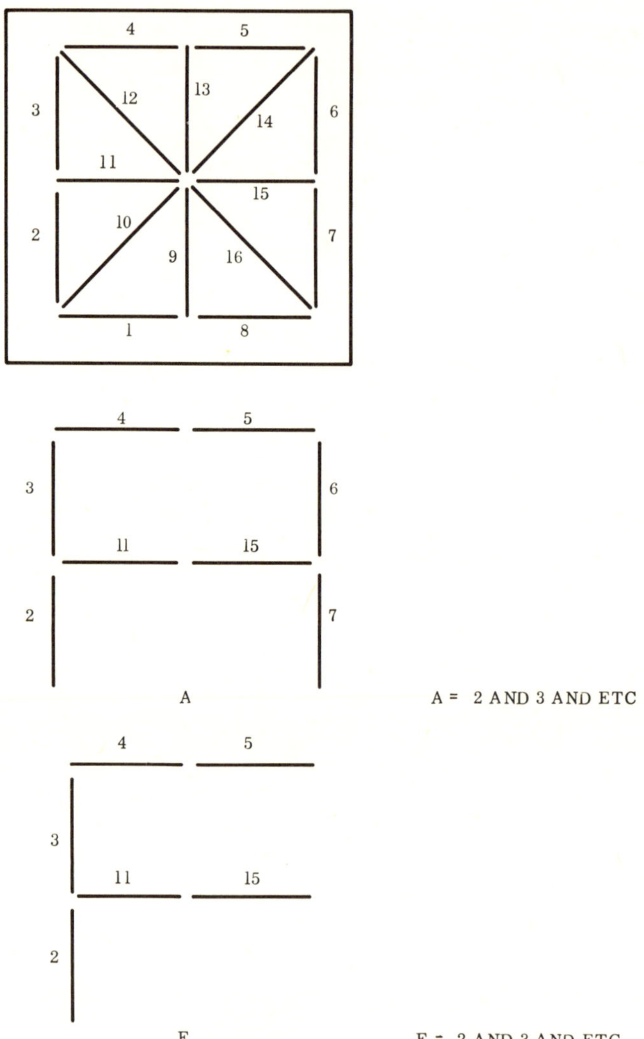

ALPHA NUMERIC DISPLAY

Figure 19–7

Recently light emitting diodes (LED's) have been used in alphanumeric displays as they require very little current to operate. Either line segments or a 5×7 dot matrix may be used to form characters on LED displays.

The control of alpha-numeric tubes presents an interesting logic design problem. While the experimenter would have to use 12 separate control lines for a numeric device, he would require $26 + 10$ (plus the number of special symbols) lines to control an alpha-numeric.

Furthermore, each main control line will have to go to one or more segments of the display. Obviously if the same segment is connected to many different control lines, some method of isolation must be used to prevent a segment from being illuminated through sneak paths. Figure 19–8 illustrates how isolation diodes are commonly used to achieve the required circuit isolation. Each control line must be fed to each required segment through a separate isolation diode as shown.

In many systems involving either numerics or alpha-numerics, it is convenient to use a binary coded input signal for each symbol displayed. If more than one numeric or alpha-numeric device is to be used, a binary coded decimal system is very useful, and each display will be fed by only the binary number representing the decimal character.

In these designs a logic circuit called a decoder must be used to convert from a binary number to the required outputs to illuminate the correct display

CONTROL LINES   A   F   LINE SEGMENTS
1
2
3
4
5
6
7
8
9
10
CR
SNEAK
PATH
11
BLOCKED
12
BY DIODE   CR
13
14
15
16

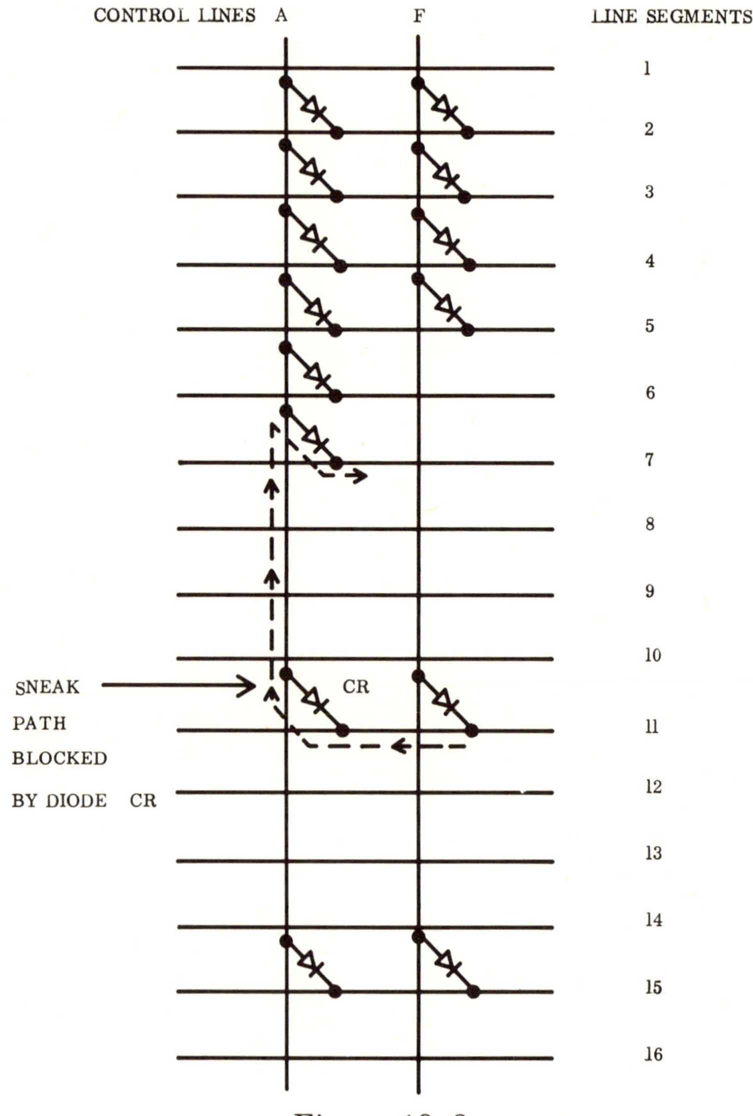

Figure 19–8

·segments. Such a decoder is illustrated in Figure 19–9.

The design of such a decoder using either a diode matrix or standard logic gates should be a trivial problem for the reader at this point. All that need be done is to consider what outputs are required for each input binary number one by one.

Fortunately this dog work is not necessary as commercial decoders are available in module form to connect between either binary coded lines or separate control numeric inputs. The *and*-to-*or* gate decoder shown in Figure 19–9 could be replaced with a diode matrix as illustrated in Figure 19–8, but a commercially available module is the practical and economical way to effect the required interface.

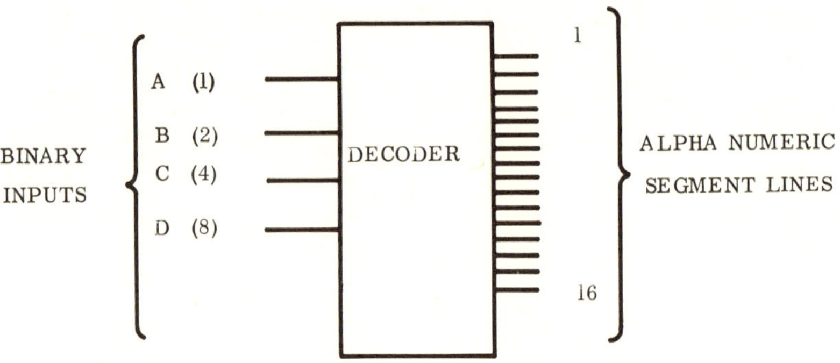

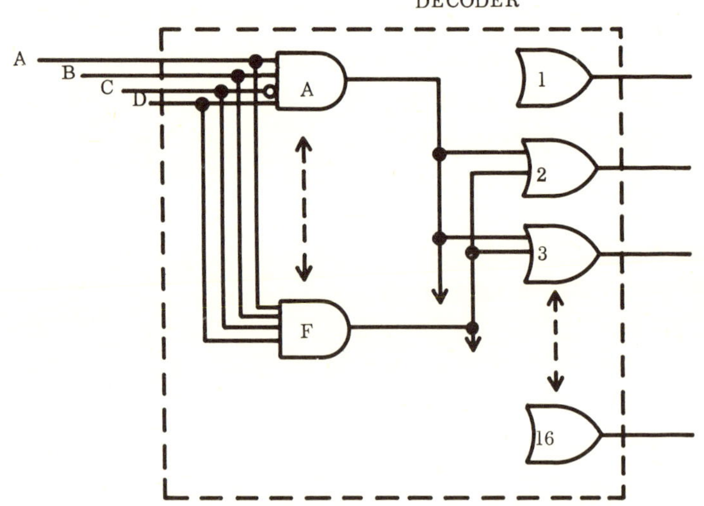

LETTER
AND GATES

LINE SEGMENT
OR GATES

(ASSUMING BINARY # 11 = A AND BINARY # 15 = F)

PARTIAL LOGIC DIAGRAM OF DECODER

Figure 19–9

Chapter 20
Sample Designs

In this concluding chapter a few practical logic system designs will be illustrated so that the reader can see how the basic principles of logic design developed in this book can be utilized to solve practical experimental equipment design problems. In no sense is this intended to be a cookbook of prepackaged equipment designs, since the whole purpose of the book is to give the reader an understanding of the theory and methodology of logic design so that he can cope with any equipment design problem that may arise in his work.

The designs were developed with a view towards illustrating the utility of the basic logic devices presented and are by no means the only way to implement the equipment requirements. The reader will find it profitable to try to figure out alternative approaches to these designs and may also find it interesting to try to improve on them (i.e., use less gates or otherwise simplify).

Figure 20–1 is a simple schematic to implement

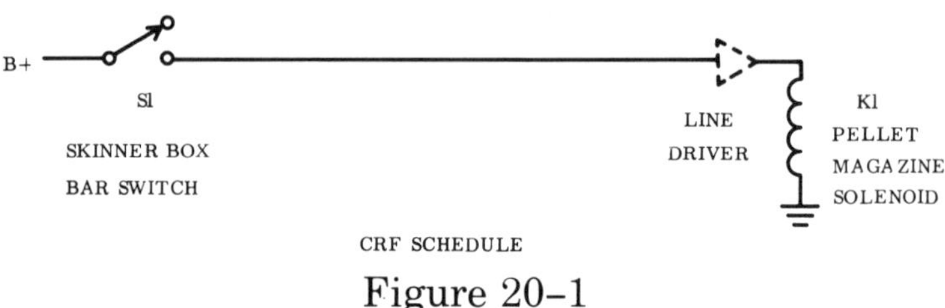

Figure 20–1

a basic CRF schedule in a Skinner box. S_1 represents the NO contacts of the switch linked to the bar, and K_1 represents the solenoid that mechanically actuates the feeder magazine. These two devices will be the basic input and output devices of all of the subsequent Skinner box control circuits discussed.

The line driver for the solenoid is shown dotted to indicate that it will not be necessary if the voltage fed through S_1 is of the correct voltage and current capability to drive the solenoid. In this case the voltage obviously should be correct, to eliminate the need for a line driver, but in all subsequent designs where a logic 1 level signal will be used to activate the output solenoid this line driver will be needed, both to compensate for the difference between the solenoid voltage and a logical 1 and/or to increase the fanout capability of the driving gate.

Figure 20–2 illustrates the implementation of a fixed ratio Skinner box schedule. Basically this circuit utilizes a counter to count sequential bar

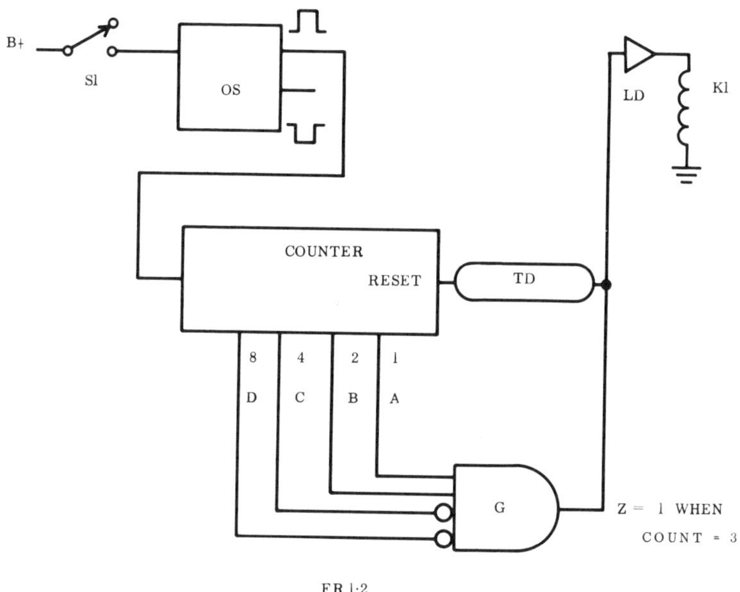

Figure 20-2

presses and a gate which converts the binary equivalent of the required count to a go signal that activates the feeder magazine solenoid.

The counter is driven by the bar switch through a one shot multivibrator to eliminate erratic outputs from the switch and assure the proper operation of the counter.

The ratio is, of course, determined by the gate logic and can be changed to any value up to 1:15 for

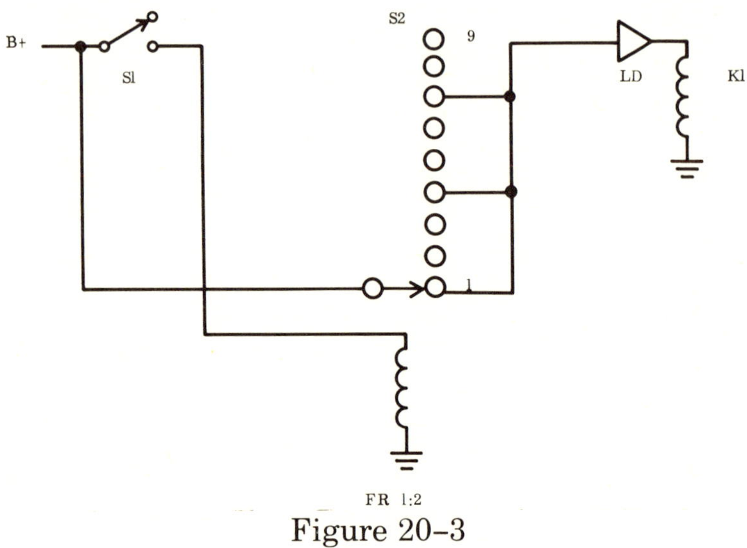

Figure 20–3

a four bit counter.

The same go-pulse that actuates the solenoid is used to reset the counter. Since the solenoid's operation takes time due to mechanical inertia, a time delay may be needed on this reset line. If this delay proves necessary, it can be provided by the use of a slow *or* gate.

Figure 20–3 shows an alternative way of providing a fixed ratio schedule utilizing a stepping switch. It is left as an exercise for the reader to implement the same function using a relay tree. (Hint: Use the output of a counter to make the relay tree step to successive output positions.)

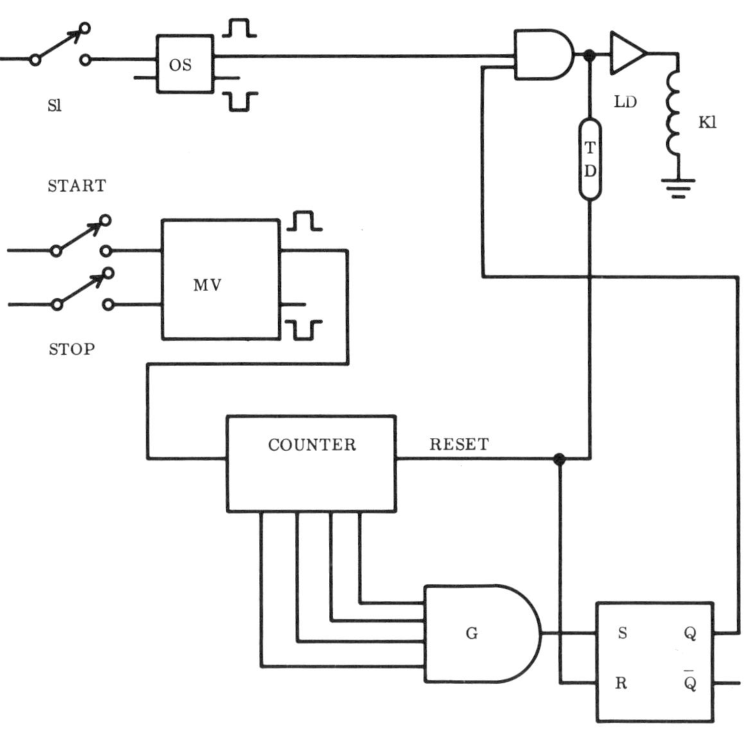

FI SCHEDULE

NOTE: GATE G SET TO GIVE 1 OUTPUT ON COUNT THAT TAKES
REQUIRED TIME INTERVAL TO COMPLETE

Figure 20–4

Figure 20–4 illustrates a method of obtaining a fixed interval Skinner box schedule. The output of bar switch S_1 drives a one shot which provides a pulse to one input of the *and* gate driving the output line driver and solenoid.

In order for this pulse to pass through the *and* gate and actuate the solenoid, the gate must be opened by the flip flop output set line being in the 1 state. This in turn requires a 1 output from gate G.

The time interval for this go output is obtained by using a counter to count the output pulses from the free running multivibrator which is used as a clock. The gate is designed to provide a go or 1 level output when the binary count of the counter corresponds to the required time interval (e.g., if the frequency of the multivibrator was 1 pulse/sec, a count of 12 would correspond to an interval of 12 seconds).

Once the flip flop is set, it will remain set until the rat presses the bar and the solenoid is actuated. The same output of the *and* gate that actuates the solenoid is also used (through a time delay) to reset both the flip flop and the counter so that the timing of the next interval can commence.

Figure 20–5 is a logic circuit that will provide a variable ratio Skinner box schedule. This design uses the basic FR circuit shown in Figure 20–2 except that a separate gate is used for each different ratio used and the ultimate output is derived from the *or*ing of these gates.

A second counter called the switch-over counter

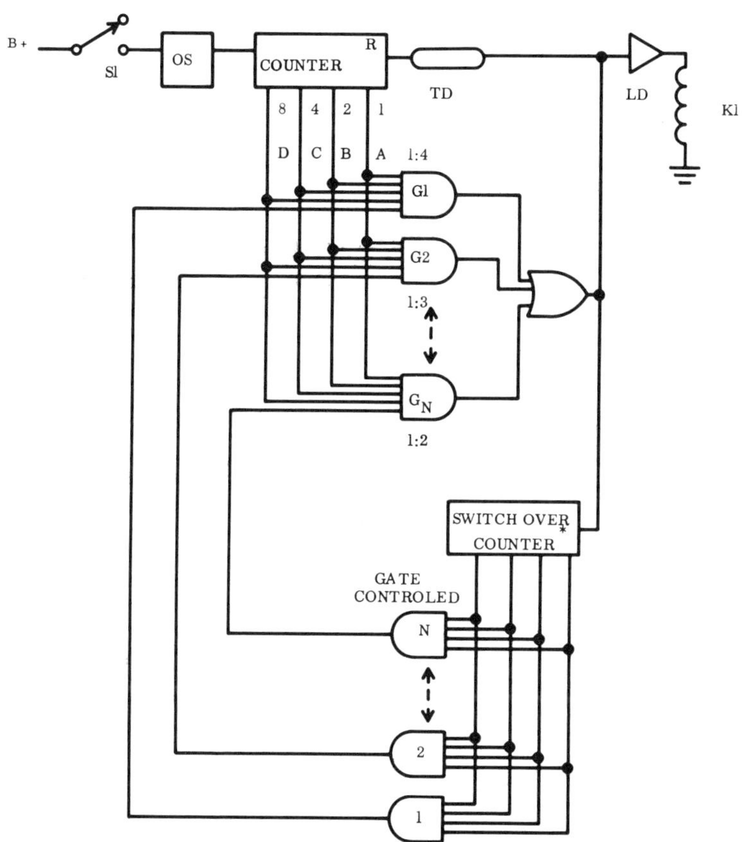

* MODULUS OF SWITCH OVER COUNTER = NUMBER OF DIFFERENT
RATIO GATES USED.

Figure 20–5

is provided which counts the number of solenoid activations obtained. This counter is provided with a set of *and* gates, and it will be noticed that each of these *and* gates controls the availability of a different one of the ratio-setting *and* gates. Hence these gates control the switching over to different go ratios during successive trials.

It is important to realize that one of the ratio gates must be available at all times; hence the modulus of the switch-over counter must not be greater than the number of ratio gates used (unless some other method is used to assure that some number of bar presses will result in a go condition).

Notice that the bar pressing counter is reset by a go signal, but the switch over counter never needs to be reset if it has the correct modulus.

Figure 20–6 shows how to provide a VI function. This circuit is basically the same as the VR system of Figure 20–5 except, instead of counting bar presses, the counter here is counting time intervals in the form of clock pulses from the free running multivibrator.

Since this is an interval and not a ratio schedule, the go condition must be delayed until the first bar press after the elapsed time of the selected interval. Thus, the gate flip flops are required to provide a memory that the required time interval has elapsed.

Again the modulus of the switch-over counter must equal the number of different intervals used or the counter must be a shortened modulus counter.

All of the foregoing illustrative designs were in

Sl
B+
START
STOP
MV
COUNTER
R
TD
LD
Kl
8 4 2 1
D C B A
1 MIN
G1
G2
.5 MIN
GN
1.5 MIN
S Q
R
S Q
R
S Q
R
SWITCH OVER
COUNTER
GATE
CONTROLED
N
2
1
VI 1 MINUTE

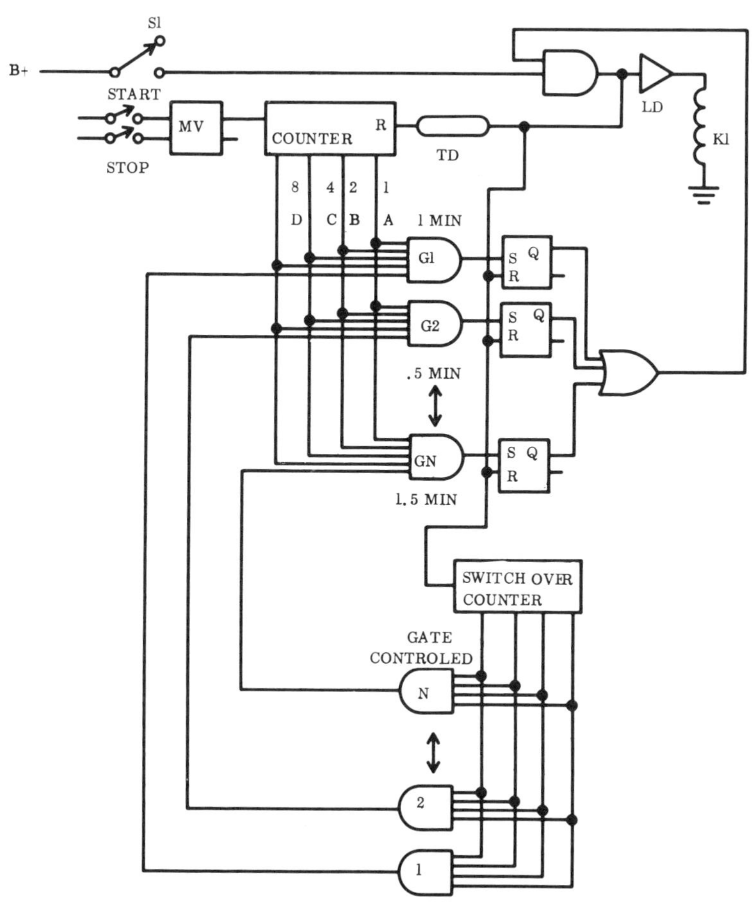

Figure 20–6

terms of *and* and *or* gates. To convert to an active gate system (nand/nor), the easiest method is to doubly negate lines.

To determine the required time delays, a timing diagram of the entire system from manufacturer's spec sheets can be drawn using the clock pulses as a reference. A simpler method is by breadboarding and "cutting and trying."

If the reader has followed all of the material presented in this book, he should now have a good theoretical understanding of the basic principles of logical devices and design. All he lacks now is the practical experience, and that will come quite rapidly as a result of tinkering with an assortment of logic modules in his own lab. The usefulness and versatility of these devices in solving practical problems is limited only by the reader's own creativity and imagination.

Appendix A

Glossary of Logic Terms

Active Device A device containing one or more sources of voltage. Most active devices used in logic design will involve the use of amplifiers made up of either tubes, transistors, or integrated circuits.

Amplifier An active device designed to convert an analogue input signal into an output signal of the same waveshape but of a different amplitude. It can also be used to increase fanout, in which case it is called a line driver.

Analogue System A system dealing with analogue variables.

Analogue to Digital Converter (A to D Converter) A device that transforms an analogue variable into an equivalent digital variable.

Analogue Variable A variable that can take an infinite number of intermediate values between two limits.

And Gate A gate implementing the *and* function. A gate that puts a 1 level logic signal out when all of its inputs are at the 1 level and a 0 level logic signal out when any of its inputs are at the 0 level. The *and* function is written $A \cdot B$ or AB.

And To Or Logic *See* Sum of Products Form.

Assertion A logic statement of an input variable or some combination of logic variables.

Basic Function *See* Basic Gate.

Basic Gate One of a set of gates from which all possible logic functions can be generated; e.g.,

Not		*Not*		*Not*
and	or	*Nand*	or	*Nor*
or				

Binary Coded Decimal (BCD) A method of representing a decimal number by giving the binary equivalent of each digit in the decimal number as opposed to expressing the entire decimal number in binary form.

Binary Number A number expressed in a number system having only two symbols, 0 and 1. A modulus 2 system of numbers.

Binary System A system dealing with variables that can have one of only two possible values at any one time.

Bistable Device A device that can stay in either one of two possible conditions for a period of time, e.g., a flip flop.

Bit Short for binary digit. A position in a binary number representing some power of 2.

Black Box *See* Component.

Block Diagram A functional representation of a system wherein the system is broken down into a set of interrelated subsystems or black boxes, but no details concerning the internal make up of these black boxes are shown. It shows the major signal flow and the major transformations produced by the system to perform its overall function.

Boolean Algebra A system of algebra designed by George Boole used to facilitate the solution of logical problems.

Branching A programing technique where there are several possible next operations and the results to the branching point determine which of the alternative possibilities is utilized. An example of branching would be when the selection of S_{n+1} is a function of the response of the subject to S_n.

Canonical Form There are two basic canonical forms that any logic statement can be expressed in:
1. A product of elementary sums (maxterms).
2. A sum of elementary products (minterms).

Cascade Applying the output of one stage or amplifier into the input of the following stage or amplifier.

Circuit Design The design of the actual electronic circuits used to implement a particular gate or logic device from basic electronic components, e.g., resistors, capacitors, transistors.

Clear *See* Reset.

Clock Any device used to establish a time base or time reference in a logic system.

Clock Pulse   A precisely timed pulse derived from a clock oscillator and used to control sequential operations in a logic system.

Clocked J-K Flip Flop   A flip flop combining the J-K and synchronous mode of operation. Thus a synchronizing pulse is needed to render the J or K lines effective in toggling the flip flop.

Coder   A device converting one sequence of binary numbers into a different sequence in accordance with some prearranged transformation formula.

Complement   The negation of a logic quantity.

Component   A subsystem of a larger system. A unit that performs some part of the overall system function or some intermediate function.

Conjunctive Function   The *and* function.

Constant   A signal which has only one value at all times.

Constraints   Those combinations of input states for which the output function could be either a 1 or a 0 without adversely affecting the operation of the overall system. Very analogous to a wild card in poker.

Counter   A device that sequentially changes output states as a function of successive input states in accordance with some rule.

Crystal Controlled Oscillator   An oscillator whose frequency is precisely controlled by a quartz crystal.

Cycle   A complete sequence of events which keeps recurring.

Cycle Counter   A counter which records one complete cycle of events and then stops until re-started.

Decade Counter A counter composed of a series of decimal counters each representing a different digit in a decimal number.

Decay Time The time it takes for a decaying pulse to fall from its peak value to 10% of its peak value.

Decimal Counter (DC) A modulus 10 counter. One with a shortened modulus that recycles after the count of 9.

Decimal Number A number wherein each digit position represents some power of 10. A modulus 10 number system; i.e., one utilizing 10 different symbols.

Decoder A device that performs the inverse operation of a coder.

Delayed Flip Flop A flip flop that requires a synchronizing pulse to render a set or reset signal effective. An RST flip flop.

DeMorgan's Theorems A set of two identities establishing the relationships between: (1) nand and *or* gates, and (2) nor and *and* gates:

$$(1)\ \overline{AB} = \overline{A} + \overline{B}$$
$$(2)\ \overline{A + B} = \overline{A} \cdot \overline{B}$$

Designation Number (#) A sequence of 1's and 0's derived from the standard basis which represents or designates a unique output logic function. Each bit in the designation number represents the condition of the output for the corresponding combination of input conditions in the standard basis.

Digital to Analogue Converter (D to A Converter) A device that transforms a digital variable into an equivalent analogue variable.

Digital System   *See* Binary System.

Diode   A device that inhibits the flow of an electric current in one direction while it freely permits it in the opposite direction.

Disjunctive Function   The *or* function.

DPDT   A double pole, double throw switch or relay contacts.

DPST   A double pole, single throw switch or relay contacts.

Dual (D)   A second function performed by the same piece of hardware when changing from positive to negative logic or vice versa. A dual is not an equivalent function. It is a different function performed by the same component.

Dual Ranked Flip Flop   A flip flop device utilizing two cascaded basic flip flops each controlled by a pair of *and* gates. This configuration provides a J-K mode of operation without the need for internal time delays.

Elementary Product   A logic product wherein each of the input variables or its negation is represented once and only once; e.g., in a four input system $A \cdot \overline{B} \cdot C \cdot \overline{D}$ is an elementary product. An elementary product is also called a minterm.

Elementary Sum   A logic sum wherein each of the input variables or their negation is represented once and only once; e.g., in a four input system

$\overline{A} + B + C + \overline{D}$ is an elementary sum. An elementary sum is also called a maxterm.

Equivalent Function Two logic functions are equivalent if and only if they have identical designation numbers.

Exclusive Or Gates A gate that implements the *exclusive or* function; i.e., a gate that gives a 1 output when either input signal, but not both, is a 1 and gives a 0 output in all other cases. The *exclusive or* function is written $A \oplus B$.

Fall Time *See* Decay Time.

Fan Out The number of unit loads that a logic or other device is able to drive.

Feedback A portion of an output signal that is applied to the input of a device.

Flip Flop (FF) A bistable device that can remain in one of two possible output states until changed, i.e., set or reset.

Fourier's Theorem The principle that any recurrent complex wave shape can be resolved into an equivalent series of harmonically related sine waves of appropriate amplitude and phase relationships.

Free Running Multivibrator A device which differs from a flip flop in that it continuously cycles back and forth between two possible output states, thereby yielding a square wave output of constant frequency.

Function The transformation performed on the input or inputs of a device to yield the output. Some logic operation or combination of operations.

Gain The ratio of output to input amplitude of an amplifier.

Gate A general term for a device to implement a basic logic function.

Gated Ripple Counter A shortened modulus ripple counter. The term "gated parallel counter" would be redundant because due to their nature all parallel counters contain gates or logic circuits to control their flip flops.

Go Conditions The conditions precedent to get a 1 level output from a logic control device.

Hardware The physical devices used to implement logic functions. The actual circuitry used.

Hard-Wired A permanent connection between two points.

Heat Sink A piece of heavy metal that can be temporarily clipped between a joint to be soldered and a logic device to prevent the heat of the soldering iron from reaching the device and damaging it. Heat sinks must be used when soldering the leads of integrated circuits.

Hybrid Form A logic statement that is expressed neither in a SOP nor POS form.

Hybrid System A system composed of both binary or digital and analogue components. The most common type of control system.

Identity A logic statement of equality that is universally true; i.e., it is true for all possible values of the variables.

Idiot Proof To design a circuit so that no possible combination of switch closures or other operations can damage the system. This is an important part of the design of any system, especially if it is to be used by inexperienced personnel.

Implication   A implies B if A is a subset of B; i.e., if every element of A is represented in B. This is written $A \rightarrow B$. If A implies B, B doesn't have to imply A. If it in fact does, then A must equal B.

Inclusive or   *See* Or Gate.

Input   A signal put into a device. The signal that is to be transformed by the device to yield the output in accordance with the function provided by the device.

Integrated Circuit   A circuit built by special techniques and automatic processes as opposed to one made by the interconnection of discrete basic components. Integrated circuits are made by utilizing a sandwich of different materials to perform the functions of transistors, resistors, etc. These devices are of subminiature dimensions and are low in cost, even for quite complex circuits.

Integrator   A device that performs the mathematical operation of integration; i.e., one in which the output level is a function of the time duration of the input.

Interface   To connect together two or more devices. The term includes whatever transformations are necessary to render the interconnected devices compatible.

Inverter   A device that performs the function of negation.

Isolation   Preventing the interaction between two or more circuits or devices.

Isomorphism   Similarity of form; e.g., $Y = 2X + 3$ and $Z = 2W + 3$ are isomorphic or of similar form. After the first equation has been solved, the solution of the second is obtained directly.

J-K Flip Flop   A flip flop featuring the J-K mode of operation.

J-K Mode   A mode of flip flop operation wherein it is permissible to energize both the set and reset lines simultaneously. This will result in the toggling of the flip flop from whatever state it is in. In an RS flip flop, this input condition is not permitted.

1 Level   The voltage used in a circuit to represent the logical 1 level.

0 Level   The voltage used in a circuit to represent the logical 0 level.

Line Driver   An amplifier used in logic systems having a unity gain whose sole function is to increase the fanout of a device.

Logic Addition   The logic operation performed by an *or* gate.

Logic Design   The design of a system in terms of logic operations without regard to the specific circuitry to be utilized to implement these logic operations.

Logic Diagram   A conventionalized representation of a logic statement using symbols of basic logic gates. A logic diagram shows how input signals are converted step by step into output signals.

Logic, μ   *See* Integrated Circuit.

Logic Multiplication   The logic operation performed by an *and* gate.

Logic Statement   A specification of a sequence of logic operations on one or more variables.

LSB   Least significant bit. The extreme right digit in a binary number.

Master-Slave Flip Flop   *See* Dual Ranked Flip Flop.

Matrix   A configuration of horizontal and vertical lines jointed by dots at appropriate positions. The vertical lines represent minterm *and* gates. The horizontal lines at the bottom of the matrix represent output function *or* gates. The upper part of the matrix is a representation of the standard basis. *See* Figure 9–5.

Maxterm (M)   *See* Elementary Sum.

Memory Device   A device that records the condition of a variable over a period of time.

Minterm (m)   *See* Elementary Product.

Module   A small physical entity representing a portion of a system. May be plug-in or have pigtail leads for soldering.

Modulus   The number of unique symbols used in a numbers system. Also the highest ordinal number that a counter can attain.

Monostable Flip Flop   *See* One Shot Multivibrator.

Multiple J-K Flip Flop   A J-K flip flop controlled by a pair of *and* gates having more than one J and K line.

Multivibrator   A general term for a circuit that has only two possible output states that it shuttles between. A flip flop is a special (i.e., bistable) type of multivibrator.

Nand Gate A gate implementing the nand function. An *and* gate with the output line negated. The nand function is written: $\overline{AB}$.

NC The normally closed contacts of a switch or relay.

Negation The operation of inverting logic levels (i.e., $A \rightarrow \overline{A}$) or interchanging 1's and 0's in a designation number.

Negative Logic When logic 1's and 0's are represented by voltage levels, with the more positive voltage representing the 0 logic level.

NO The normally open contacts on a switch or relay.

No Go Conditions The conditions under which the conditions precedent for a 1 level output from a logic device are absent.

Nor Gate A gate implementing the nor function. An *or* gate with the output line negated. The nor function is written: $\overline{A+B}$.

One Shot Flip Flop A flip flop which has only one stable output state. When toggled this device changes state and then returns to the rest state after a definite period of time. Hence, it is used to generate a fixed time duration pulse.

One Shot Multivibrator *See* One Shot Flip Flop.

Or Gate A gate implementing the *or* function. A gate that puts out a 1 level signal when any of its input lines or combination of input lines have a 1 on them and puts out a 0 when all of the input lines have a 0 on them. The *or* function is written: $A + B$.

Or to And Logic   *See* Product of Sums Form.

Oscillator   A device used to generate a recurring waveshape (usually sinusoidal) at a given frequency.

Output   A signal coming out of a device. It represents the inputs as transformed by the function performed by the device.

Parallel Counter   A counter wherein each flip flop changes state at the same time in going from one state of the count to the next.

Passive Device   A circuit having no internal source of voltage. Thus it cannot involve such devices as amplifiers, inverters, electron tubes, or transistors. Usually limited to the circuit elements of R, L, and C, or devices resolvable into these elements.

Positive Logic   When logic 1's and 0's are represented by voltage levels with the more positive voltage representing the 1 logic level.

Power Supply   A device used to supply the dc voltage required to operate all gates in a system. This supply voltage is never shown on logic diagrams although it appears on schematics or wiring diagrams.

Product of Sums Form (POS Form)   A logic statement in the form of a logic product of two or more logic sums, e.g., $(A + B)(B + C)$.

Program   A predetermined sequence of operations performed by a system.

Pulse A signal characterized by going from a 0 to a 1 level for a fixed period of time and then returning to the 0 level. An ideal pulse would be square or rectangular in shape. Pulses may be single or recurrent either regularly or irregularly.

Pulse Shaping Refers to the squaring up of the edges of pulses that have passed through a series of passive gates or the conversion of some other signal into a pulse or series of pulses. Pulse reshaping occurs automatically in all active gates.

Pulse Width. The time interval between the start and stop of a pulse. Measured between the first and last voltage levels that will function as 1 level logic signal.

Recursive System A system where part of the output is fed back to the input, usually after a time delay.

Relay A switch actuated by an electromagnet. This device is capable of the remote control of switching and converts electrical rather than mechanical energy into switch closures.

Repetition Rate (Rep Rate) The number of pulses per second.

Reset The condition of a flip flop when the Q output is at the 0 level.

Ripple Counter A counter wherein the component flip flops are cascaded so that a signal must sequentially pass through each flip flop when recording a new count.

Rise Time The time it takes the leading edge of a pulse to go from 0 to 90% of its peak value.

RS Flip Flop The basic type of flip flop. One having a set and a reset input line, only one of which may be energized at any one time.

Schematic Diagram A diagram showing the actual circuitry involved in implementing a logic function or gate, but not showing how the actual point to point wiring is laid out.

Schmitt Trigger A device that puts out a logic 1 level signal for as long as its input voltage exceeds some preset threshold value.

Set A group of elements. Also the condition of a flip flop when the Q output is at the 1 level.

Shift Register A device that remembers a sequence of binary digits and that moves each digit recorded over one place as each new digit is added into the register.

Shortened Modulus Counter A counter counting fewer events than the number of flip flops used would permit it to before it recycles.

Signal Some voltage level standing for something else. An input or an output that is thought of as flowing through the gates of a system sequentially.

Signal Conditioning Transforming of a signal into another signal in accordance with some rule. Pulse shaping or squaring is a special type of signal conditioning.

SPDT A single pole, double throw switch or relay contacts.

Specification   A set of input-output statements describing the transformations wrought by the system on the inputs to produce the outputs. A set of statements precisely defining: what the system is to do, under what conditions the system is to do it, and with what degree of precision the system is to perform. The basic goals of the design.

SPST   A single pole, single throw switch or relay contacts.

Stage   A functional unit of operation; e.g., each tube in a cascaded three tube amplifier is referred to as a stage. Each gate that a signal must pass through sequentially is also called a stage.

Standard Basis   An orderly and standardized way of writing all the possible permutations of input signal states.

Steady State Signal   A signal that maintains some steady value as opposed to a transient signal. A steady state signal may vary as a function of time provided that it is recurrent, e.g., a sine wave or a dc voltage level.

Subsystem   *See* Component.

Sum of Products Form (SOP Form)   A logic statement in the form of a logic sum of two or more logic products, e.g., $ABC + AB\overline{C}$.

Supply Voltage   The dc voltage level put out by the power supply used to energize the gates in a system.

Switch   A device used to make and interrupt circuit continuity that is actuated by mechanical energy.

Synchronous Flip Flop *See* Delayed Flip Flop.

Synchronous J-K Flip Flop A flip flop combining the J-K and synchronous mode of operation.

System A group of components functioning together to produce some overall function.

Time Base Any source of time reference for a system, e.g., a clock oscillator.

Time Delay (TD) A device whose function is to delay a signal in transit. Usually a slow, cheap *or* gate, or group of *or* gates, is used for this function.

Timing Diagram A diagram showing the changes of state of different parts of a logic device as a function of time and their relationship to each other.

Toggle (Noun) A type of switch having a bat shaped handle to be actuated. (Verb) To switch or change the state of a flip flop.

TPST A triple pole, single throw switch or relay contacts.

Transient State A signal that occurs briefly during the change over from one stable condition to another.

Transit Time (δ) The time taken for a signal to pass through a gate or flip flop.

Truth Table A chart showing all possible input permutations in standard basis form and the output states of each output variable for each permutation. It is, in fact, a detailed specification for a logic device.

Type D Flip Flop An RST flip flop with the R line connected to the S line through an inverter.

Type T Flip Flop A flip flop that is toggled from

whatever state it is presently in to the opposite state by a pulse on a single input line that triggers it.

Unit Load A standard measure of the input driving requirements of a gate.

Variable A signal that can take more than one value at different times.

Weighting The assignment of different values (usually in powers of 2) to different input or output signals.

Wiring Diagram A diagram which, unlike a schematic, shows the actual junction points of the physical wiring of a unit.

Appendix B

Standard Logic Symbols

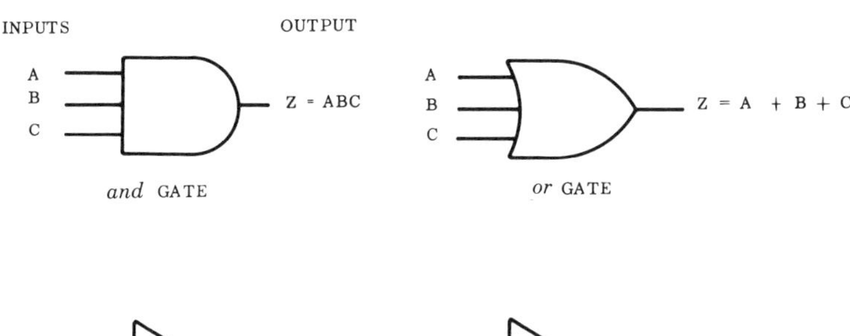

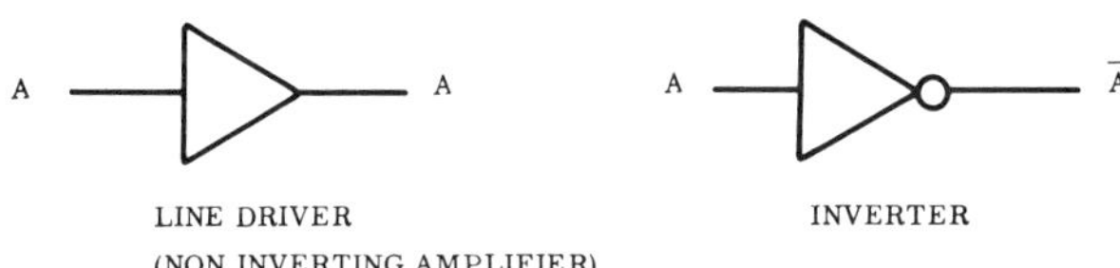

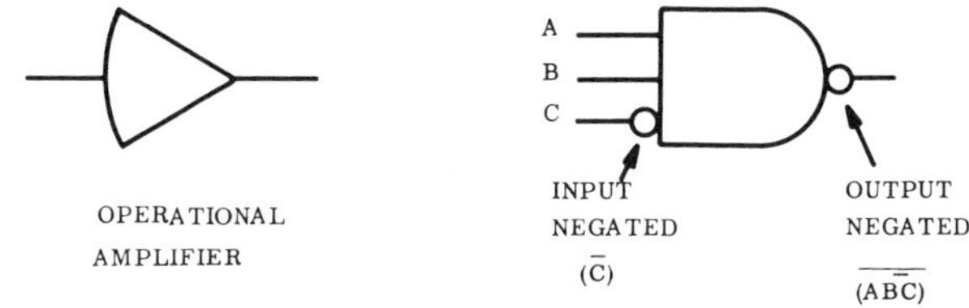

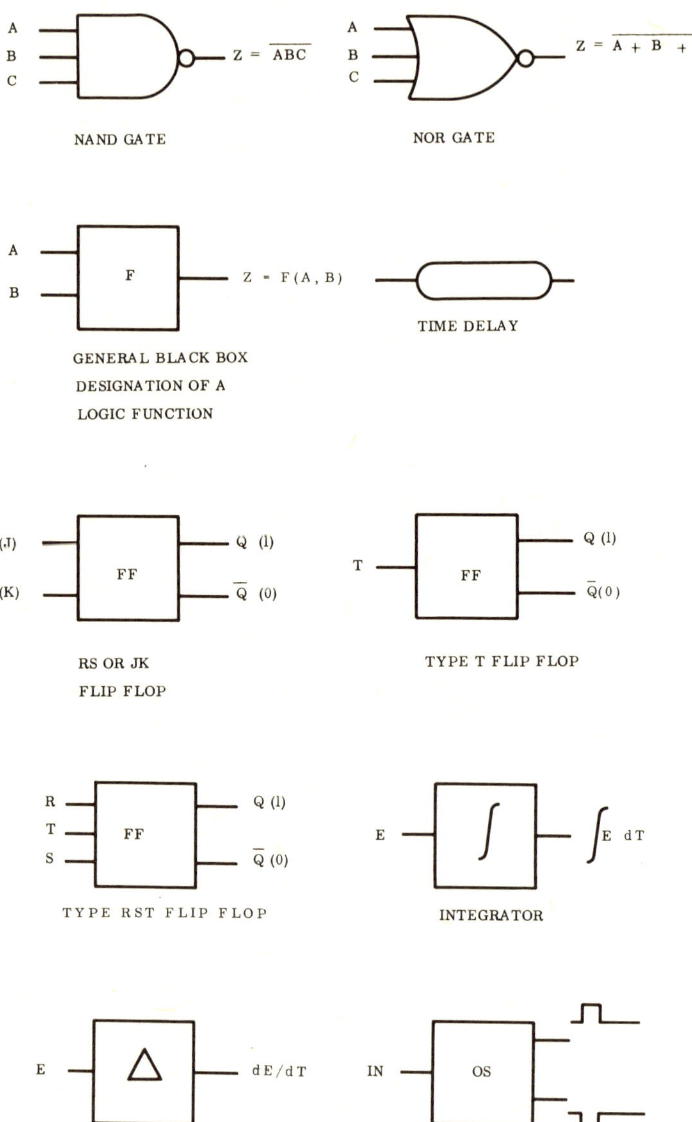
A
B
C
Z = ABC
NAND GATE
A
B
C
Z = A + B + C
NOR GATE
A
B
F
Z = F (A , B)
GENERAL BLACK BOX
DESIGNATION OF A
LOGIC FUNCTION
TIME DELAY
R (J)
S (K)
FF
Q (1)
Q (0)
RS OR JK
FLIP FLOP
T
FF
Q (1)
Q (0)
TYPE T FLIP FLOP
R
T
S
FF
Q (1)
Q (0)
TYPE RST FLIP FLOP
E
∫
∫E dT
INTEGRATOR
E
△
dE/dT
DIFFERENTIATOR
IN
OS
ONE SHOT MULTIVIBRATOR

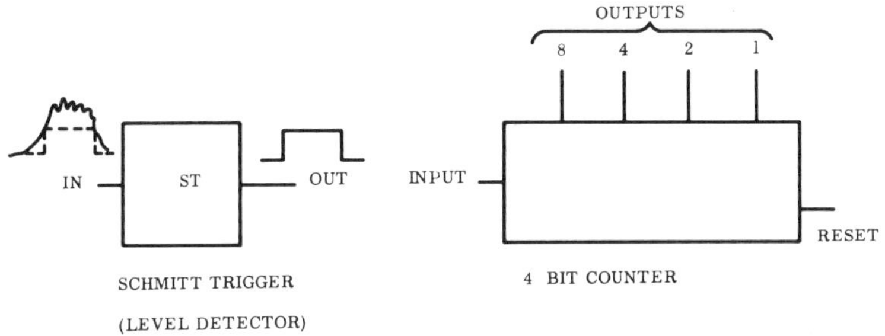

SCHMITT TRIGGER

(LEVEL DETECTOR)

4 BIT COUNTER

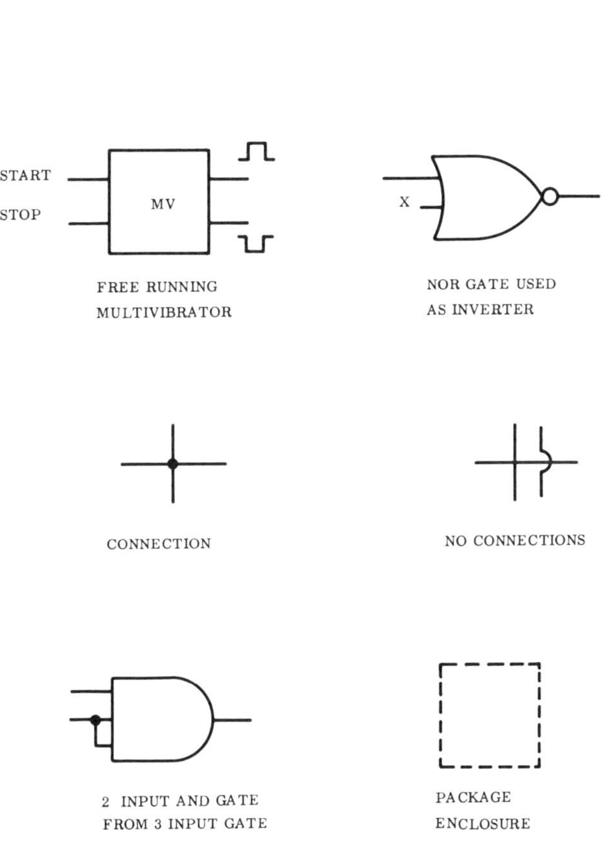

FREE RUNNING

MULTIVIBRATOR

NOR GATE USED

AS INVERTER

CONNECTION

NO CONNECTIONS

2 INPUT AND GATE

FROM 3 INPUT GATE

PACKAGE

ENCLOSURE

Index